Roy Worac
2.3.74

Beyond Belief

Beyond Belief

Haunting - Poltergeists - Possession
Clairvoyance - Precognition

Brian Branston

Weidenfeld and Nicolson
London

Contents

Author's Note

It is the practice of authors to name and thank people who have helped them and then to absolve their helpers from any conclusions the writer may choose to draw.

Many people have helped me both in my investigations and in the drawing of my conclusions. But because the subject of this book is really about contact with a force or forces which no conventional scientist will even postulate, let alone recognize – forces which appear to be able to manipulate physical matter and even space and time – an open believer runs the risk of being labelled crazy. For this reason I simply say 'thank you' to those who have helped me. They know who they are and they will understand.

BRIAN BRANSTON
28 September 1973

Illustrations

1
The Possession of
Mrs Hockley

A book which sets out to persuade reasonable people that there is a case for not dismissing out of hand apparitions, poltergeists, possession, clairvoyance, mind-reading, precognition, stigmata, spirit photographs, ectoplasm, and suchlike oddities ought to be based firmly on testable evidence. I have to admit at once that my early experiences of what is sometimes called psi-phenomena are sadly lacking in evidence that would stand up in court. I can only aver that this is what I saw, this is what I heard – but at least my testimony is first hand and not hearsay.

There are reasons why I was careless at the start about collecting evidence which might support a belief in psi-phenomena. I am talking now of the years immediately after the Second World War. My main interest lay not in the phenomena themselves, but in what they had to offer as radio programme material. If they were no good for programmes, or my bosses refused to be persuaded they were, then I had to drop them; for I had more than enough other work and worry to cope with. Because of this situation, I was so short-sighted as to allow the one piece of evidence in the case of the possession of Mrs Hockley to pass clean out of my hands and disappear.

Since the evidence turned on Mrs Hockley's claim to be the loud-speaker, as one might say, for spirits who spoke African dialects, mid-European languages of Slav origin, and ultimately Urdu, I shall need to begin my story a little way back.

1

In early 1945 the Germans were being bludgeoned into surrender and the Japanese war was drawing to a close. For over four years I had been soldiering in India and Burma and most of the time I had served with Indian troops, mainly Punjabi Muslims, Pathans and Baluchis from the mountain valleys of the North West Frontier. A few days after arriving in Quetta in 1941, I engaged a *munshi* or teacher to give me lessons in classical Urdu. As I moved from one station to another I simply swapped *munshis*. By the time I was posted back to England in 1945 after taking part in the last Burma campaign, I spoke Urdu pretty fluently, I was clued-up on Indian affairs, could eat the hottest curries and had a liking and respect for both Hindus and Muslims.

My home posting instructions from a jungle 'nowhere' about 100 miles south of ruined Akyab in the Arakan told me to report at Chittagong, Calcutta and Madras where I was to await final orders to go to a transit camp at Deolali before shipment from Bombay to England.

The details of my journey are not relevant to this particular narrative and apart from one incident I will skip over them. In crowded Madras I was staying in the annexe to the Connemara Hotel, whiling the time away with spells of swimming in the pools of the Gymkhana Club or the more august Madras Club, redolent of the passing Raj with its obsequious dark-skinned 'bearers' and their deferential 'Yes master ; no master' and of Rudyard Kipling with its tame mongoose tip-toeing about the punkah-cooled dining room.

The event I wish to recall occurred one teatime as I stepped out of a rickshaw which had dropped me at the Connemara annexe. I was accosted by a young well-dressed Sikh. He was wearing a European lounge suit topped by the usual neat tight turban of the orthodox bearded follower of Guru Nanak. His black eyes flashed. He wanted to tell my fortune.

'*Nahin mangta*', I said : 'No thanks'.

'The sahib will be very rich', he said in English. This was the conventional opening gambit designed to appeal to everyone's cupidity. I was hot and sticky and wanted a bath. My bush shirt was clammy as a dish rag. I moved to go past.

'The sahib is returning to *Vilayet*', (Blighty – England) he said. This was a fairly logical assumption at that time. 'To his wife and three children'.

I burst out laughing in his face: 'I'm not even married', I said. He stood aside with a look of puzzlement on his face.

And yet within the year I had returned to England, and before long I did have a wife and three children. Few men acquire a complete family overnight, but when we were wed, my wife had three children from a former marriage, Shirley, John and Peter. Before long we started to augment their number and eventually had three more. I often wondered whether that Sikh really had seen into my future or not. Well, it was beyond belief, wasn't it ?

With a family to fend for I had to search for a civilian job which would, if possible, fulfil at least two functions: bring in sufficient money to support five and later eight people, and give me what they call these days 'job satisfaction'. I was fortunate enough to have secured before the war good academic qualifications (some of them the more attractive, no doubt, for being a bit way-out, such as an Honours degree in Anglo-Saxon and Old Icelandic). I also had an active war-record with a formerly 'Forgotten Army', the 14th, whose reputation was enhanced by suddenly being remembered as the last fighting force still in the field. In addition, my five years of war service in usually independent commands, junior though they might be, had given me a strong streak of self-reliance and a certain amount of dash – or cheek. With this at my back I bearded the BBC in Manchester and landed what I have always regarded as (for me) the finest job in the world, that of radio producer.

Early in 1948 I was based at the BBC's Leeds studios, a former Quaker Meeting House in Woodhouse Lane, a solid chapel-like building whose outer walls were dark with the soot of the Industrial Revolution. The happy family atmosphere of the studios of those days was still maintained in 1948 with everybody (as always in the BBC) on first name terms.

Frequently you never even got to know a person's surname. I remember with affection Albert the studio attendant who still shuffles on to the 'box' wearing his apron to light the candles of television's *Good Old Days* music hall programme; Doris, the cook – a character, but oh! those dinners; Dick Gregson and Rex Tucker, the drama producers; Frank Morgan, programme engineer; Andy Weir, scriptwriter – writing an *Archers* series a year before Midland Region even got wind of it; Frank Wade, music programmes; and Barney Colehan, whose name was rapidly becoming part of one of radio's first universal catchphrases, 'Give 'im the munny, Barney!' from Wilfred Pickles's *Have a Go* quiz. My office was next door to that of Barney Colehan. All the producers' offices were situated in a row at the back of the building; they were postwar temporary lash-ups quickly knocked together of timber and plaster board to cope with the rapid expansion then going on in BBC broadcasting. As a result, you could hear every word spoken in offices either side of you. One morning about 9.30 I walked into my office and heard through the wall on Barney's side a strange, agitated woman's voice.

'Good God! What's he up to now?' I thought. It *was* a woman's voice, wasn't it? I began to have doubts, for occasionally there were deeper undertones. And although the language appeared to be English, there was a strong foreign accent. Whoever it was had it all to herself or himself. If Barney was there, he was letting the flow of words wash right over his head.

I shouted at the wall, 'Are you there, Barney?'

The voice stopped. 'Brian?' (Nobody except my wife called me Ronnie any more – my wartime name of Brian had stuck for good). It was Barney.

'Yes, Barney?'

'Come in here and listen to this . . .'

Barney had what we used to call a 'T.D.7' in his office, a waist-high record player designed to play back the acetate discs cut by BBC recordists before tape-recorders became common. The voice I had heard had come from the disc still spinning on the turntable. 'Listen to it', he said and replaced the tone arm.

It was a remarkable performance. Now obviously a woman's voice but a woman impersonating a man, and speaking in a foreign accent. The disc ran for about three and a half minutes and before asking him to put it on for a second time, I enquired who it was.

'It's a Mrs Hockley – a spiritualist medium. It was sent to me by the bloke who recorded it. He's a chap dealing in war-surplus electronic gear. He's got a recorder. Lives in Bradford and wants to know if we can use this in programmes.'

It appeared that the recordist, whom I will call Mr Briggs, had invited Mrs Hockley to go into trance in the sitting room of his home and had sat working the recorder and occasionally putting questions to the tranced medium to which she reacted immediately. Mrs Hockley, a woman of working-class origins, who had left school at fourteen and who was by this time in early middle age, may or may not have followed the political events of the post-war period. Be that as it may, the lately deceased Jan Masaryk, son of the founder of Czechoslovakia (for the voice claimed to be none other than his) was using Mrs Hockley to pass a pretty damning message to the Western World.

Whether this disc is still in existence, I do not know. It presumably went back to Mr Briggs a quarter of a century ago. But the performance on it was so affecting that I still remember it. I asked Barney to lend it to me for further listening. Before I indicate what was on the record, I should outline the political background to it.

In 1938 at Munich, British business men threw Czechoslovakia to the Nazi wolf, just as in 1933 they had abandoned Manchuria to the Japanese snake in the grass and Abyssinia to the Italian jackal. In 1947 they did it again, only this time it was the Russian bear which hugged independent life out of Czechoslovakia.

Of course, what I should have done with Mrs Hockley's Jan Masaryk disc was first, to have it transcribed, then I should have compared it with recordings of the live Jan Masaryk, subjecting it to a detailed study. But I did none of these things,

5

thinking perhaps that it was all too difficult, time-consuming and even then likely to prove inconclusive ; but most of all, I reckoned I could put Mrs Hockley to a better test over which I could exercise control.

So I treated the Masaryk recording in a much too off-handed way, and can now only give an indication from memory of what it was all about. The voice began by warning the West that if Britain, France and the USA continued their present course of abandoning Czechoslovakia to the Communist elements, then Russia would take over and Czechoslovakia would cease to exist as an independent nation. This message was, I suppose, pretty obvious to any student of events, but was it so obvious to a Bradford working-class woman who may or may not have read a daily newspaper ? We know now that the message fore-told the truth, but did any of the Western politicians of the day subscribe to it strongly enough to do much about it ? The answer is, of course, no.

The more sensational passage in the Masaryk recording stated that far from committing suicide by jumping from the window of his room in the Foreign Office, the speaker had been flung to his death: murdered. And it was obvious who the murderers were – the men who at the instigation of the Russians had brought about the Communist coup.

The events surrounding the Communist *coup d'état* are as follows. In a letter dated 24 February 1949, President Benes of Czechoslovakia gave way to the coup organised by Gottwald and wrote 'You know my sincerely democratic creed. I cannot but stay faithful to that creed, even at this moment, because democracy, according to my belief, is the only reliable and durable basis of decent and dignified human life'.

Gottwald had issued a call three days before, on 21 February, which resulted in Communist-dominated 'Action committees' being set up in all parts of the country. Within a few days these committees had infiltrated all sections of national life in Czechoslovakia, had carried out arbitrary purges of political opponents, press, government offices, education and cultural institutions, had received official recognition from the new government and by the end of February had established virtually dictatorial control over all political, economic and cultural activities.

On 26 February the American, British and French governments made a joint statement issued by the US State Department condemning the new regime as a disguised dictatorship and accusing the Communists of seizing power through 'a crisis artificially and deliberately instigated'.

Previous to these events, on 11 September 1947 an unsuccessful attempt had been made on Jan Masaryk's life when bombs were sent through the post to him and two other non-Communist ministers.

Now on 10 March, the Czechoslovakian Government announced that Dr Jan Masaryk the Foreign Minister and son of the first President of the republic had committed suicide by throwing himself from a window of his apartment in the Czechoslovakian Foreign Ministry (the Czernian Palace) in the early hours of the morning. The official announcement ran: 'On 10 March 1948 in the early morning, the Minister of Foreign Affairs, Dr Jan Masaryk, voluntarily ended his life, filled with labour for the Fatherland and the Nation. As a result of his illness, combined with insomnia, he evidently decided in a moment of nervous breakdown to end his life by jumping from the window of his official apartment into the courtyard of the Czernian Palace. The day before his tragic end, and also during the evening, Minister Masaryk did not show any evidence of mental depression, but on the contrary, was full of active life and of his usual optimism!'

The new communist Prime Minister, Gottwald, said in a funeral oration delivered on 13 March, 'Our dear Jan' had been driven to suicide by an 'organised campaign from the west . . . . It has been a terrible blow to me and to all his friends'.

That these were crocodile tears seemed evident to many in the West. Ernest Bevin said in the British House of Commons, 'We do not know really what has occurred, except that he has passed'. Another British politician, Herbert Morrison, described the events in Czechoslovakia as 'horribly similar to the

Hitler technique', adding that the overthrow of Czechoslovakian democracy was the work of 'men who owe loyalty not to their own country but to a foreign power'.

It is obvious therefore that the tenor of what Mrs Hockley's Jan Masaryk was saying appeared to many people to be correct; though I don't think that any reputable commentator went so far as to say what Mrs Hockley's possessor was saying, namely that Masaryk had been murdered and that his murder was really at the instigation, if not with the direct participation, of the Russians.

When Mr Briggs sat making this recording in his drawing room with Mrs Hockley in a private trance, he got so caught up with the drama of the message, that he could not forbear calling out in a strong Yorkshire accent, 'If you are Jan Masaryk (he pronounced the 'J' as in John) then speak to us in Czech!'

At once Mrs Hockley's possessor broke into a torrent of what could have been 'Czech' or (for all I know) gibberish. It was remiss of me not to have had it tested. Even if it had been 'Czech', a language unlikely to have been learned by a woman of Mrs Hockley's background, still it would not have constituted absolute proof of her communicant being Jan Masaryk. Nevertheless, the outburst suggested to me a plan which might afford proof of Mrs Hockley's authenticity or otherwise.

I telephoned Mr Briggs and asked him if Mrs Hockley would give me a private seance. He said he would find out.

He came back to me with her acceptance and the proposal that a seance should be held at his home so that he could record it. He invited my wife and me to dinner and when I put it to Dodo she was rather frightened at the idea of a spiritualist seance and asked if she couldn't bring a friend, a Mrs Hinchley, our bank manager's wife in Pateley Bridge. And so it was arranged that we should all go.

Mr Briggs said he would pick us up from the Leeds BBC Studio on the evening of the seance and drive us to his home. In those immediate post-war days life was pretty austere, food rationing and petrol rationing were still with us, so we were all surprised when Mr Briggs turned up that evening driving his own Rolls Royce. From a gold cigarette case he offered us cigarettes with his own name printed on them in gold. And his subsequent hospitality matched his style.

We met Mrs Briggs and Mrs Hockley at his home and after drinks sat down to dinner.

I now have to make another shaming confession. I don't really know if her name *was* Hockley. I never saw it written down, and because Mr Briggs spoke the true West Riding speech, which ignores aitches, for a long time I thought the lady's name was Ockley. It may even have been Otley. But in recent years I have come to the conclusion that it really was Hockley.

She was a dumpy, solid, round-faced lady in early middle age. Anything less ethereal or spirit-like it would have been difficult to envisage. She was *solid,* and seemed to have both feet firmly on the ground. Over dinner my own two ladies were nervously giggly, Mrs Hockley seemed to be eager for the coming test, and I liked her more and more. She believed firmly in her 'guides' – this became patently obvious and she wanted them tested and found true. One story told against herself disarmed suspicion: apparently her most persistent guide was a departed physician called 'Dr Jim'. He would force himself upon her at the most inconvenient times. One night she and her husband had gone to bed when she felt the presence of Dr Jim. I gathered that Mr Hockley, an ordinary working man, did not share his wife's spiritualist enthusiasm, and on this occasion was already dropping off to sleep when Mrs Hockley fidgeted in the bed and asked plaintively whether, just for once, Dr Jim wouldn't clear off and leave the pair in conjugal peace. Mr Hockley was, understandably, as he might have put it, 'pretty bluddy fed up' and made no bones about saying so – even if Dr Jim should happen to hear him. At this, Dr Jim's nearness became so oppressive that Mrs Hockley actually felt the pillow go down on her side of the bed.

She sat up in her curlers and switched on the light. There on the pillow by her side lay her big black tom-cat. Because it was summer, the bedroom window was open, and the cat had simply walked in.

As I say, one couldn't but be disarmed at her willingness to tell such a story against herself. She was convinced enough of the authenticity of her guides even to have them laughed at. But Mr. Briggs and I had planned a real test after dinner for Mrs Hockley.

Before we left the table Mrs Hockley brought up the subject of a particularly horrid murder because, she said, she wanted me to check with the police concerned to confirm that through clairvoyance she had told them where to search for the bodies of the victims. It was the notorious double murder in 1935 of Isabella Van Ess and Mary Rogerson.

To summarise the case: a Parsee, Dr Buck Ruxton whose real name was Bikhtyar Rustomji Hakim, who had graduated Bachelor of Medicine at Bombay and London Universities, was convicted at Manchester Assizes on 13 March 1936 of the murder of his Scots mistress, Isabella Van Ess (formerly married to a Dutchman) known as Isabella Ruxton.

The case had gruesome features, the more gruesome then, in 1935-6, than might appear today after more than a generation of private and public atrocities blatantly displayed in newspapers, magazines and on television. Ruxton suspected his mistress of infidelity and the pair continually quarrelled. On 14 September 1935 Isabella Ruxton left their home at 2 Dalton Square, Lancaster to drive to Blackpool in the doctor's Hillman Minx. She intended to meet her two sisters and form a party to see the noted attraction of the North, the Blackpool Illuminations. At 11 p.m. that Saturday night, the three sisters said their goodbyes, Isabella Ruxton drove away leaving the bright lights behind her and simply disappeared. She was, as they say, never seen in one piece again.

Back in Lancaster, at 6.30 next morning, a Sunday, the Ruxtons' charlady, a Mrs Agnes Oxley, was surprised to receive a visit from Dr Ruxton who told her not to bother coming round to the house that day (as she usually did at 7.15 a.m.) because Mrs Ruxton and their nursemaid Mary Rogerson had gone away on a holiday to Edinburgh.

Later that same morning, Ruxton turned away a patient and a tradesman, apologising for his dirty hands and saying that he had been taking up carpets. At half-past eleven he called at the home of a friend accompanied by his three children and asked for them to be looked after during his wife's absence. His right hand was bandaged and he explained that he had cut it that morning opening a tin. In the afternoon, Ruxton asked a Mrs Hampshire, one of his patients, to come to Dalton Square to clean down 'ready for the decorators coming . . . . . in the morning'. She noticed that the bath was a 'dirty yellow . . . I gave the bath a good scrub with hot water and Vim, I could not get the stains off'. When Mrs Hampshire tried cleaning some rolled-up, badly stained carpets by throwing on buckets of water 'the colour of the water that came off was like blood'. On the Monday, 16 September, Ruxton hired an Austin Car with which on 17 September he was involved in a collision with a cyclist at Kendal in the Lake District. He told a policeman that he was returning from a business trip to Carlisle. In the meantime, and up to 20 September, two other charwomen at Ruxton's home, Mrs Smith and Mrs Curwen, found a great many bloodstains about the house as well as an unpleasant smell. Mrs Curwen was sent out for Eau-de-Cologne and a syringe, and Ruxton sprayed the house.

On 29 September, the broken-up remains of two female bodies were found in a ravine near Moffat in Scotland. A newspaper wrapped round some of the bits like butcher's meat became a damning clue. It was a 'slip' copy of the national weekly newspaper the *Sunday Graphic,* a 'slip' being one of a limited number of inserts containing local news for a certain area – in this case, Lancaster and Morecambe. The Chief Constable of Dumfries contacted Lancaster Borough Police and Ruxton's game was as good as up – especially when a blouse and a pair of child's rompers found with the body parts were identified as coming from Ruxton's home.

On 13 October Ruxton was charged with the murder of Mary Rogerson the nursemaid ; and on 5 November with that of his mistress Isabella Ruxton.

The remains had been literally carved up. They consisted of two skulls, two torsos, seventeen parts of limbs and forty-three portions of soft tissue. All characteristics capable of identifying both ladies had been removed including finger prints and in one case, both eyes. Mary Rogerson was known to have a squint which was taken to be the reason why the younger woman's eyes had been cut out. Life-sized photographs of Isabella Ruxton and Mary Rogerson were superimposed over pictures of the skull remains and found to match. It appeared that the older woman had been strangled and both bodies had been dismembered and drained of blood soon after death.

Dr Ruxton was convicted of the murder of Isabella Ruxton and hanged at Strangeways Jail, Manchester on 21 May 1936.

As I have said, Mrs Hockley claimed that through clairvoyance she had been able to give information to the police which led to the discovery, in a very out-of-the-way spot, of the two bodies. She mentioned a police inspector whose name I did not trouble to remember and suggested that I apply to him for confirmation of her story. Once again, I have to confess that I did nothing about it at the time. That evening at dinner I was really only concerned with one thing and that was the coming seance with Mrs Hockley.

We all moved into the drawing room. My wife and Sally Hinchley told me afterwards that they felt intensely nervous, inclined to pant and with their knees knocking. I myself felt expectantly excited. We spectators sat on easy chairs in the form of a horseshoe with Mr Briggs and his recording gear at the toe of the shoe. Mrs Hockley sat on a stiff-backed chair in the middle of the open end of the shoe. The lights were not turned off or dimmed.

Mrs Hockley sat quietly, her plump feet barely touching the carpet. Occasionally she muttered ; her eyes closed ; and she appeared to be pushing something away with her right hand. Sometimes I could hear her say, 'Go away. No, I don't want you now, *dear*!' and I gathered that spirit-guides were queueing up to be made manifest orally through their medium.

She opened her eyes wide, turned her head to the right and looked at me. She said 'There's somebody standing behind you!'

After the initial shock of looking round and finding empty

space I said, nervously, 'Oh yes ? Who is it ?'

Mrs Hockley said, 'Does the name Bathurst mean anything to you ?'

'Bathurst ? I don't know anybody called Bathurst.'

'You wouldn't know him. He's been dead 300 years. Does the name Trinity College mean anything to you ?'

'Trinity College ? Trinity College Oxford, Cambridge – might be Dublin ?'

'It's Trinity College Oxford. He's wearing a funny hat and there are strips of fur on his gown.'

'Well,' I said, 'what does he want ?'

'Nothing. He's just looking after your interests!'

There was a pause ; Mrs Hockley said, 'I've got Dr Jim here. He wants to come through . . . .' ('*He* would', I thought, but didn't say anything). She held a muttered unintelligible conversation with, I presumed, Dr Jim.

'Dr Jim says you have something wrong with your feet!'

The imparting of this information gave me a shock. There were only two people in the room who knew that there was something wrong with my feet, and Mrs Hockley wasn't one of them – the other was, of course, my wife. During my service in India I had contracted a fungus disease sometimes called 'jungle foot', 'Singapore foot' or simply 'foot rot'. Little if anything was known of a cure. At one time, I remember it well, my unit was at Seringapatam, the capital of Tippoo Sultan with its romantic associations with the opening chapters of *The Moonstone*, and my feet were so bad I could not walk and had to be carried. The little round-faced Indian medical officer of our regiment treated me, cleaning out the pus from between my toes. It was a painful, irritating ailment and for a long time afterwards I had to hobble with a stick. The treatment at the time was to drench the affected parts with a red liquid called Castellani's Paint, and to give the toes as much air as possible. This wasn't a cure, simply a suppressive, so I came back to England expecting to have foot rot for the rest of my days. Now, out of the blue, here was Mrs Hockley passing on a message about my feet from Dr Jim. It was just that, passing on a message – she was not speaking or attempting to speak in what might have been Dr Jim's own voice: 'Dr Jim says he's going to cure your feet!'

What could I say ? I replied, 'Please thank him very much,' without being in the least convinced that I was going to be cured. And yet, (to jump ahead) within a few months I was cured, whether Dr Jim was instrumental or not. I had transferred from Leeds to work at the BBC in Belfast and we had bought a house at Dundonald in Co. Down. One day Dodo went into the village chemist's shop and asked for a cure for foot rot. She came away with a tube of ointment which, before I had used half the tube, had cured the disease. Coincidence ? Dr Jim ? I personally wasn't worried, but in memory of Dr Jim I pass on the name of the preparation to any other sufferer : it was *Bioform*.

To return to Mr Briggs' drawing room and Mrs Hockley sitting stiffly in her upright chair. For a while she was quiet, her eyes closed. Then she began to drum with her feet on the floor. She stood up and went into a sort of African dance, the kind of rugby-club-after-the-match 'eye-ga-zig-a-zumba.' This was too much for me, I could not remain seated and I got to my feet and joined her in the dance. Occasionally she let out a stream of some strange language – of course, it could have been African tribal speech; I had no means of checking. She grew tired and we both sat down.

When Mrs Hockley seemed to have come to herself again I broached the subject of my proposed test. Because she seemed to have a facility for languages it had occurred to me that I could personally test her in one, namely Urdu, which for her at that time must merit the adjective esoteric. Today, in Bradford, the scene is different with a large immigrant population of Punjabis, whether Muslims or Sikhs. But in 1948 it was unthinkable that Mrs Hockley could have mugged up Urdu. In addition, a notable Indian character had that year 'passed on' as the spiritualists say, and I determined to ask Mrs Hockley to go into trance, establish contact with the person in question and let him talk to me in Urdu. It was, of course, Mahatma Gandhi.

I put the question directly to Mrs Hockley, 'Do you think

you could go into trance and establish contact with Gandhi ?'
She said she would try.

Before I relate what happened, I will summarise relevant
information on Gandhi from the *Encyclopedia Brittanica* and
Keesing's Contemporary Archives. Mohandas Karamchand
Gandhi was born in one of the Indian princely states of
Kathiawar on 2 October 1869. His family was well-to-do, both
his grandfather and father being chief ministers in the state.
During his lifetime Gandhi became revered as a holy man – a
Mahatma. He constantly opposed British imperialism but did
it through passive resistance: he abhorred violence. Like
another holy man who preached peace, brotherhood and the
turning of the other cheek, he came to a violent end. On 30
January 1948, in New Delhi, while on his way to his usual
evening prayer-meeting, Mahatma Gandhi was assassinated.
As he walked from Birla House to the lawn at the back where
the prayer meeting was to be held, Gandhi was approached by
a Hindu fanatic who broke through the crowd, took a pistol
from his pocket and fired three shots. Gandhi cried, *'He
Rama*! Oh God!' and fell. He had received severe wounds in
the chest, stomach and groin. He was carried into Birla House
and died half an hour later. The murderer was a Hindu,
Nathuram Vinayak Godse, editor of a small Hindu Nationalist
newspaper published in Poona and violently opposed to
Gandhi's policy of communal tolerance and especially Hindu-
Moslem amity. On 31 January Gandhi was cremated.

Mrs Hockley then, was about to try to get into communication with Gandhi.

I watched her closely from my easy chair. She sat upright
with her arms resting on her thighs. She closed her eyes. She
began to breathe very deeply. This 'over-ventilation' is one of
the recognised aids to going into trance.

Two things then happened which surprised me. The flesh
appeared to fall away from her plump face and her nose became
quite thin and peaked. A bluish tinge suffused the area around
her mouth and for all the world she took on the appearance I
had been so familiar with in India of a middle-aged Hindu.
Next, she suddenly put the toe of her left shoe behind the heel

of her right shoe (tightly laced, I noticed) and with a quick thrust flung the right shoe across the room towards Mr Briggs who was busily recording the procedure. In a flash, her left shoe followed.

She got stiffly to her feet, eyes still closed, and began scrabbling at her dress with both hands as though trying to rip it off. She muttered words to the effect that she wished to divest herself of Western clothes and wind herself in the sort of sheet that Gandhi used to wear.

She turned directly towards me, took a couple of steps forward and dropped on to her knees at my feet as I still sat in the easy chair. I leaned forward. She did not open her eyes but suddenly clutched with both hands her bosom and cried in a loud voice, 'Shot! Shot!'

My wife and Sally Hinchley were watching with mouths agape and I myself was pretty moved – even more so when Mrs Hockley suddenly grasped both my hands in hers and I could feel from the trembling how intense was her emotional state.

In a husky whisper she said to me, 'It is very difficult to come to you through the fire!'

'Who are you?' I asked rather lamely.

Her face and lips contorted with strain as she tried to say something. Her attitude was exactly like a stutterer attempting to stammer out a communication.

I tried to help her. 'Are you Gandhi?' I asked. She nodded. 'Then if you are Gandhi', I said, 'will you speak to us in Urdu?'

Her reply was a dry whisper: 'It is very difficult for a Western tongue'.

'Try', I said. All the time her speech was like something from the grave . . . She struggled as before and her hands gripped mine even harder.

I said 'If I speak to you in Urdu will you answer me?' She nodded.

Immediately I said slowly and deliberately, '*Apka nām mujhē batayiē!*'

The air rattled in her throat and her lips seemed to be forming sounds like repeated M's and K's. I could make nothing of it. She had not replied to my question; at least, not in a way that I could understand. I thought she had failed the test.

My question translated simply means 'Please tell me your name', and all she had to say in reply was 'Gandhi'. Afterwards it did occur to me that she might have been trying with her repeated M's and K's to say his full name of Mohandas Karamchand. However, a little later Mrs Hockley snapped out of her trance and the seance broke up. Mr Briggs drove Sally Hinchley, Dodo and me back to the studios having made me a present of the acetate disc on which the 'Gandhi' communication had been recorded.

It had been a surprising experience, but, as I believed, a total failure in vindicating Mrs Hockley as a person able to communicate with the dear departed.

Next morning in Woodhouse Lane I took the disc into the small Studio 2 to play it back and invited the two drama producers, Dick Gregson and Rex Tucker, to hear it with me. Barney was away at the time. Both Gregson and Tucker were greatly impressed with the professionalism of Mrs Hockley's performance. They said they had never before experienced so expert a creation of death in a voice.

But for me on hearing the play-back, there was something else much more startling.

The question I had put to Mrs Hockley the night before had been couched in a form of Urdu used only to evince extreme politeness. It's the sort of form that would correspond in English only to an archaic speech such as 'Would'st thou tell me thy name?' If I had been talking to one of the men in my old unit I would have used the common form for 'tell me your name' which is *'Tumhārā nām mujhē bātō,'* and not *'Apkā nām mujhē batayiē'*. Yet as I listened to the play-back in Studio 2 I heard myself put the question slowly, with pauses between the words; only before I could say the last one, *'batayiē'*, Mrs Hockley herself said it!

This I had not noticed at the seance. But the recorder had picked it up and the disc had faithfully retained it. If Mrs Hockley had been able to memorise odd phrases of Urdu it

17

could only have been 'soldiers' ' Hindustani and would scarcely have included a word form like '*batayiē*'. In any case, she had said it before me.

What is the explanation ? Telepathy ? Mind reading ? Even if that is all it was, that is remarkable enough. But – I am not so sure.

Some months afterwards, when I was working as a talks producer in Belfast, I was telling a group of friends and colleagues one lunchtime in the canteen about my experiences with Mrs Hockley. A few weeks afterwards one of those present, Ursula Eason, then Assistant Programme Director, came to see me and said, 'I've found out who your Bathurst is!'

'No!' I said.

'Yes', she replied and went on to give me the details.

The President of Trinity College Oxford in 1664 was one Ralph Bathurst. He was born in 1620 at Hothorpe in the parish of Thedingworth near Market Harborough in Northamptonshire. He was one of a family of seventeen, fourteen of whom were sons and six of whom were killed fighting for Charles I. One of Ralph's brothers was Benjamin, father of Alan, First Earl of Bathurst. From 1673-6 Ralph was Vice Chancellor of Oxford University.

Now, where would an uneducated woman like Mrs Hockley have come across information about Ralph Bathurst in her everyday life? Not impossible – even to the suggestion of a mortar board or similar 'funny' academic cap and a gown with fur bars. Not impossible, but I would have thought it extremely unlikely. At any rate, some day, when I have time, I propose searching the records around about Hothorpe in the parish of Thedingworth – for according to family tradition some of my family's forebears came from those parts. I wonder if any of them ever crossed paths with Ralph Bathurst ? And if, indeed, his spirit had reason for 'watching over my interests' ?

2
The Spook of
Ardara Avenue

Because I had lived and worked in Ulster before the war and liked it, I transferred in 1949 to the BBC in Belfast and we moved as a family to a large detached house in Ardara Avenue, Dundonald, County Down. In the old days, there used to be a famous racing circuit here, the 'Ards Circuit' and the Belfast-Newtownards road, once part of the race-course, ran across the bottom of our avenue. The famous Dundonald turn was a mile nearer the city by the pub and the trolley-bus terminus. Ardara Avenue is a short cul-de-sac leading from the main road and situated about a mile from the Belfast city boundary. We were surrounded by open country, that lovely green rolling grassland of County Down, not six miles from the head of Strangford Loch and ten minutes run by car from Scrabo, that miniature mountain with its stone tower, once the home of the King of the Leprechauns: well, so they said in their charming Irish way.

We took over Ardshee (I won't give the house its proper name) in the summer of 1949 after living for a month at the seaside resort of Bangor to allow us time to search for a permanent home. We all loved Ardshee from the moment we moved in: its rooms were spacious and well proportioned, there were plenty of them, there was a fine sweep of drive up to the front door and a large garden back and front where the children and their half-bred Airedale dog Tigger could play safely. At the

19

time Shirley was fourteen, John ten, Peter eight, Tim nearly two and Philip about six months.

Before long we were joined by Mathilde, a Swiss girl – well, she was as old as Dodo and me, about thirty-four – who had been working as an au-pair for a titled lady and wanted a change. Mathilde came from the German-speaking part of Switzerland, the Bernese Oberland, and she was plump and comfortable like the women of that area. She was methodical and meticulous, always spick and span, and on duty would insist on wearing a maid's white apron and bib.

Mathilde's main job was helping to look after the two babies, Tim and Phil; the other two boys, John and Peter, were well able to look after themselves. They were in fact young devils, always up to some high-spirited mischief or other.

'Yez'll need to watch thon bhoys, Mas' Bran'son', the road sweeper told me one day. 'I seen 'em swingin' hand to hand across the road under the railway bridge . . . It's a twenty foot drop!'

'I'll speak to them, Pat,' I said 'And thank you'.

One day that autumn I caught them sneaking past the garage to the back door with their pullovers held up on their bellies and bulging with apples. 'Where did you get those apples?'

They stood shame-faced. Peter, the youngest, looking up with large innocent eyes, said, 'Everybody does it, dad. We've been scrumping – farmer so-an-so's orchard. All the kids at the Nissen huts do it.'

'Get back at once!' I said, 'Give farmer ―― his apples and don't come to me again without bringing a written receipt from him!'

They returned an hour later minus apples and handed me a grubby sheet of lined paper with the message in pencil: 'Dear Mr, I received the apples. Thank you and oblige. Yours faithfully Mr ――.' Well it was suspicious but I let it pass. I'd made my demonstration and it wasn't until years afterwards that they told me how they'd shared the apples with a widow-woman down at the Nissen huts who had obligingly written the note for them.

20

With two such boys at large, we never knew what was going to happen next, and by the same token, any untoward happening was first laid at their door. We had no hesitation in blaming them for the bent needles.

With such a squad of small children Dodo was never without some sewing. There came a time when she complained to me that whenever she went to her sewing basket she found herself hampered by the needles being bent.

She showed me a couple. They were evenly bent like a drawn bow. 'You've been pushing too hard through too many thicknesses of material.' I said. She denied it. 'Bad steel, then ; you can thank the war for that.' She bought fresh new packets and left them in her workbasket. When she came to use them, although the paper packets appeared untampered with, the needles were bent.

'It's John and Peter,' I said, 'must be. Who else could it be ? Not the young 'uns.'

We taxed the mischief-makers with this latest example of their activities. They denied it strenuously and because they were not usually afraid of owning up, our suspicions were shaken.

I took one of the larger needles from a new packet and made to bend it between the thumbs and forefingers of both hands. It snapped. I tried another. That snapped. You just could not bend the thin tempered steel. It always broke.

We looked at some of the old needles which were bent for signs of heat – that tell-tale blueing which would have let us know that somebody had taken away the temper. No suggestion of it.

It came to this : if Dodo wanted to do any serious sewing she had to buy a new packet of needles and use them straight away.

Next, it happened to the knitting needles. These being of softer steel there was no real difficulty in bending them. But we never caught anyone red-handed. It was a mystery, and remained so for a long, long time.

Years afterwards, when I told the story to Dr Eric Dingwall, the celebrated psychic investigator, he was very interested : it was he who first made me think that there might be more in the bent needles than met the eye. What that 'more' was, may be best discussed later after I have mentioned some other odd happenings.

At the time when they occur the happenings usually do not appear so odd as perhaps they really are. For instance, take the tobacco smoke. Both Dodo and I smoked cigarettes in those days, but no one in the house smoked a pipe. Yet Dodo, who has one of the keenest noses of anyone I know, noticed the aroma of pipe tobacco smoke – not in the house, but always on the square patio outside the french doors leading to the garden.

Our neighbour on that side was Joe Douglas, a quiet, grey man, a Principal in the Ministry of Agriculture at Stormont. But Joe didn't smoke a pipe. The scent was strong and usually in the daytime when both John and Peter were at school and I was at work. This ruled out the two obvious scapegoats and explains why I myself do not remember having smelled the tobacco smoke.

But Dodo was quite certain that the scent was there: always on that little sheltered patio with the brick wall on the left up which had been trained a profusion of sweet peas. You'd have thought that the scent of sweet peas would have drowned out anything else. But it didn't.

Perhaps we ought to have connected the aroma with the spook. But we tended to dismiss what happened because it was so ordinary and our lives with five children to cope with were so full anyway.

Occasionally, in the evenings, Dodo and I would help Mathilde to bath the young ones, put them to bed in the nursery whose walls I had decorated with scenes from *Pinocchio*, and then, leaving Mathilde in charge, take the car down to the picture-house halfway between Dundonald and Belfast. We did this one night in the winter, arriving back at Ardshee in the dark at about eleven o'clock. We both stepped out of the car, I to unfasten the garage door alongside the house and put the car away, Dodo to walk on in to prepare our 'bed-night' cocoa. The house was in darkness, Mathilde having gone to bed. The porch doors were plate glass squares from top to bottom and were fastened with a Yale lock. The inner doors were similar. These led to a wide hall with a dining room on your left, the drawing room on your right and the stairs facing you. The stairs went up on the dining room side, the left, and in between them and the drawing room the hall ran on to the back of the house. Turning left under the landing of the stairs you came to a door which led into a breakfast room.

I suppose I was about two minutes behind Dodo in entering the house. She had switched on the hall light and I followed to where I expected she would be, in the kitchen, which you reached through the breakfast room I have already mentioned.

She was, in fact, standing beside the open door under the stairs leading to the breakfast room. She had switched on the light. She told me that as she switched on the light she saw a man sitting in a low armchair immediately opposite to her by the side of the fireplace.

The vision had been momentary. The light went on: the man was there: then he was gone.

She had no sense of fear and we dismissed what she had seen as a trick of the light, made our cocoa and happily went to bed.

Some months later when the days were beginning to draw out, I myself walked from the kitchen, through the breakfast room, under the stairs into the hall and as I turned to face the glass doors at the far end, I saw the spook.

Again, the vision was momentary. The house door faced roughly west and the last light of the setting sun was in the sky. Silhouetted against the glass doors was the standing figure of a man wearing a trilby hat. Because the light was behind him I could make out no detail of clothes or dress. I was conscious only of a shadowy man. Then, in an instant, he was gone.

So I walked on to the door but there was nothing there. The summer wore on and one hot August day I had come home from work and gone upstairs to take a bath. The bathroom was at the front of the landing and situated over the front door. Our bedroom was to the left of the bathroom as you approached it and had a large bay window, facing west over the Nissen Huts

at the bottom of the avenue and beyond green fields, farmer
——'s orchards and the tower of Dundonald village church
peeping above the brow of the hill. It was so hot when I came
out of the bath that I sat stark naked in a chair looking at the
peaceful scene through the window of our bedroom. I was
there, I suppose, for about twenty minutes.

Suddenly I heard Dodo running up the stairs. She came into
the bedroom. 'You devil!' she said, 'why were you teasing
me ?'

'What do you mean ?' I said.

'Running up the stairs like that to escape me. I heard your
trousers swishing.'

'But I'm not wearing trousers,' I said, 'I've been sitting here
starkers for the last twenty minutes.'

So this time she had not seen the spook but heard him.

That summer my widowed mother came to visit us from
England. We told her nothing about our ghost, in fact we discussed him with no one, not even Mathilde and certainly not
the children. After my mother had been with us for some days
and when I was at work, she asked Dodo who the strange man
was who had passed her on the stairs ? Who she thought 'he'
was I do not know but since there was no physical presence we
came to the conclusion that she had seen our spook.

We were never able to unravel this mystery and I don't know
how one would start. We had bought the house together with all
the furniture from a widow lady, whose husband was a Wing-
Commander in the air-force but who had died shortly before
in the house. One usually connects ghosts with dead people:
could it have been our widow's husband ? You don't like to
question people on such subjects. Apart from the intimacy of it,
they are apt to think you are crazy. In any case, she had
emigrated to South Africa immediately the house sale was
completed. I have never seen any other ghost, nor has Dodo.
We never even discussed the matter with my mother so, as far
as she is aware, she has never seen a ghost in her life.

It is tantalizing and baffling to leave such a visitation
unexplained. However, I hope to be far more forthcoming on

24

the subject of spooks in chapter 5[1] when I shall have more general evidence to help in forming a reasonable assessment. In the meantime, I may conclude with some observations on the subject of the bent needles.

Most people who find themselves beset by odd happenings do not realise that the kind of phenomena they are experiencing have frequently happened before, all down the ages, and to many an unsuspecting victim.

A reputable citizen of Bristol, Mr Henry Durbin, experienced some very strange happenings at the Lamb Inn (without a drink taken) in particular on 15 February 1762.[2] These happenings centred on the Landlord's young daughters Molly and Dobby Giles. Durbin writes:

As I had many reflections thrown on me in the public papers, I was determined to try an experiment, in order to have a certain fact to convince the world, if possible. I made Molly sit down in a chair in the middle of the parlour; I took a large pin and marked it at the top with a pair of scissors; I put her hands across and bid her not to move. I desired the above gentlemen (witnesses) to watch her narrowly; none were in the room beside ourselves. I then put the marked pin in her pincushion in which the other pin was; I put the pincushion that hung at her side into her pocket-hole and pulled her clothes over it. As I moved one hand (my watch being in the other to see the time) she cried out she felt somewhat at her pincushion, and directly was pricked in the neck, (her hands still being across). The identical pin I had marked was run through the neck of her shift, and stuck in her skin, *crooked very curiously*.[1] It was not a minute from the time I put the pin in to her being pricked in the neck. Those two gentlemen were witnesses to the fact. We then marked four other pins, and I put them in her pincushion singly as before; and *all of them were crooked*[3] and stuck in her neck. I

[1]See page 115.
[2]*A Narrative of Some Extraordinary Things that Happened to Mr Giles' Children*, Bristol 1800.
[3]My italics.

examined the pincushion (after we took every pin out of her neck) and found the pins gone from the pincushion.

What Durbin was calling attention to was the fact that Molly was being pricked by pins which apparently moved without human agency. Nevertheless, in passing, he noticed that all the pins were bent, or as he puts it 'crooked very curiously'. Reading his experiences again reminds me that I too tried an experiment back at Ardshee with a knitting needle. I took a new straight needle out of a packet and secretly laid it inside the top of the picture rail in the hall. I said nothing to anybody and when I came to remove it a week or so later, it was bent!

Durbin was dealing with two little girls who were the foci of poltergeist activity. I have often wondered whether the bent pins might not have been the beginning of some such activity centred on our teenage daughter Shirley. She was very unhappy during her first year in Northern Ireland. She did not settle down in her school and (I believe) began to dread attending. Her unhappiness started to express itself physically and she suffered from a chronic gastric upset – not serious, but frequent enough to make her life miserable. Much as we disliked it, we at last decided that she would only improve if she returned to England and we sent her to live with my mother, and attend my old school, Penistone. It was another of the reasons why we made up our minds to return as a family to England, which we did about eighteen months later. But by then the 'bent needles' had stopped.

3
Poltergeist

The country folk of Europe have been familiar with the pranks of the poltergeist for centuries. The word itself comes from old German folklore and means noisy, knocking, bumping, throwing spirit. John Milton alludes to its mischief in *L'Allegro* where 'she was pinched and pulled, she said, and he by Friar's Lantern led'. Well, Friar's Lantern may be easily explained away on a dark night as ignited puffs of marsh gas, methane : but nobody so far has explained the pinchings and pullings and other manifestations of the poltergeist or, given they do exist, what causes them.

Do these manifestations exist objectively or are they only figments of a disordered imagination ? Here's what Mrs Marcia Howells, a twenty-two-year-old housewife from Swansea said to a television news reporter in 1965 : 'Well it was about five o'clock in the evening and I had just poured my little girl a cup of tea in my mother's room. I went out the kitchen and when I opened the door this bottle came flying towards me, and of course I shut the door to protect myself. I opened it again and see this other bottle, so I picked up the children and I ran out of the house. As I ran out, my husband was coming down the street here, and he ran straight in the house and by the time he'd gone in there – all the place was turned upside down!'

This was the year 1965 and the statement was by a person who was at the centre of the happenings. Here is another poltergeist account, almost exactly 300 years earlier, by two eyewitnesses, Joseph Glanvil, a clergyman, and Squire Mompesson, a magistrate. The events were associated with

27

Beyond Belief

Squire Mompesson's children and in particular with one of his daughters, aged ten. Mompesson, in an attempt to get to the bottom of it all, lodged his other children out and moved the ten-year-old girl into his own bedroom, but the manifestations would not be got rid of, and began every night as soon as the little girl was in bed. The case is a famous one and has come to be called 'The Demon Drummer of Tidworth', for 'people heard the beating of a drum, while altogether it would beat Roundheads and Cuckolds and several other points of war, as well as any drummer'. There was a variety of other noises made manifest such as the pattering of peas falling on the floor and those sounds associated with the shoeing of horses. Squire Mompesson reported:

> It returned with mighty violence and applied itself to my youngest children, whose bedsteads it would beat when there has been many of strangers as well as ourselves present in the room, that we did at every blow expect that they would have fallen to pieces. Then it would run under the bedsteads and scratch as if it had iron talons and heave up the children and the bed and follow them from room to room and come to none else but them.

The Rev Joseph Glanvil, FRS, wrote of his encounter in January 1663 with the Demon Drummer of Tidworth. The Mompesson children went to bed and at about 8 p.m. a maid reported that it was at it again. Squire Mompesson took Glanvil and a third gentleman upstairs to the girls' bedroom where they found two little girls aged between seven and eleven modestly in bed. A strange scratching noise came from behind the bolster but the girls' hands were:

> out over the Cloaths, and they could not contribute to the noise that was behind their heads. They had got used to it, and ... seemed not to be much affrighted ... I searched under and behind the Bed, turning up the cloaths to the Bed-cords, graspt the Bolster, sounded the Wall behind, and made all the search that possible I could to find if there were any

28

trick, contrivance or common cause of it, the like did my friend but we could discover nothing ... After it had scratcht about half an hour or more it went into the midst of the Bed under the children, and there seemed to pant like a Dog. I put my hand upon the place, and felt the Bed bearing up against it ... I looked under and everywhere about, to see if there were any Dog or Cat ... but found nothing.[1]

A few years after this, in the English university town of Cambridge on a site where the Divinity School now stands, a poltergeist was raging. It was 1695 and according to the account:

there came by Mr Isaac Newton, a very learned man, Fellow of Trinity College, and, seeing several scholars about the door, 'Oh ye fools!' says he, 'will you never have any wit? know ye not, that all such things are mere cheats and impostors. Fie! Go home for shame!' and he would not go in.[2]

But perhaps Mr Isaac Newton was not as broadminded as he would have others be. Having seen his apple fall, and having postulated his theory of gravity, he found himself the object of scorn and attack by brother scientists, for having theorised an occult force, gravity, into existence. Why, however, should we stop at one such force? As a brother Fellow of Trinity College said 300 years later in a television broadcast:

Do the scientists really know all the forces that there are in nature? When I was young they admitted of only two – magnetism and gravity. Now they tell us there are two more – the atomic forces, the strong and the weak interaction. All this must, I think, make the layman ask 'Is this the lot, or are there not other powers at work in the Universe?' But the scientists are right in requiring us only to believe in things for which there is real evidence.[3]

[1]Joseph Glanvil *Saducismus Triumphatus*, London 1681.
[2]Quoted by Dr George Owen in a BBC Television broadcast 24 April 1967.
[3]Dr George Owen as before.

29

'Only to believe in things for which there is real evidence'. This has always been my aim, and when in 1967 the case of Mrs Marcia Howells' poltergeist and others came to my notice, it seemed to me that Dr George Owen who said those words was my man. Dr Owen is a small, quiet spoken, bright-eyed Welshman, Fellow of Trinity College Cambridge and at the time I first met him, university lecturer in genetics – in other words a scientist himself ; today he is the Director of the New Horizons Research Foundation, Toronto, Canada. Dr Owen is the author of the definitive work on poltergeist phenomena *Can We Explain the Poltergeist?* published 1964 in the USA and never (the loss is ours) published in Britain.

I went to see Dr Owen in Cambridge and asked if he would help not only with a poltergeist film but also with one on what appeared to be a haunted hall (the subject of the next two chapters) and he agreed.

For the purposes of our film we decided to concentrate on three modern poltergeists, one of which was currently 'raging'. We would therefore be able to include not only first hand eye-witness accounts, but in the case of the current poltergeist at a council house in Northfleet, Kent, actually take cameras and recorders to the troubled house. Of the other two, one was very recent – that of Mrs Marcia Howells ; and the second, that of Virginia Campbell of Sauchie, Scotland, had been personally investigated by Dr Owen, though not until the phenomena had virtually stopped.

I have already quoted from a news interview given to a television reporter by Mrs Howells. Some months after this interview I asked my colleague at the BBC, Bob Saunders, to go to Swansea and film Mrs Howells. Here is her verbatim account of what happened at her mother's home in Rhondda Street:

Mrs Howells: It was about three days after we moved into Rhondda Street, my husband and I we went to bed and we woke up feeling as if somebody was choking us. My husband he opened the windows, went downstairs to see if any gas had been left on but nothing like that had happened. So we went to bed and thought no more of that.

Then my husband always locks the doors before going to bed and one night I had to go downstairs and the door was open. So I locked it, went back to bed and told him he didn't lock the door, but he said he had. Then when we went downstairs in the morning the door was open again. These things happened over a period of months.

Then one afternoon I was having tea with my mother in her room and it was on a Monday, and she said that she had to go across the shop, so I said 'All right'. I said, 'I'm going to my room now to do a bit of work'. So as I went out, the children came down the passage behind me and I opened the door of my room and I seen a bottle rise off the mantelpiece. I thought I was seeing things so I, seeing the bottle coming towards me, shut the door to protect myself, and the bottle smashed against the back of the door! So I opened the door again, and I seen another bottle rising off the mantelpiece. So I just shut the door and picked up the children and went and waited on the doorstep for my mother to come home. So she came back and I told her what had happened, so she said to me, 'Oh don't be so daft!' she said. So we went into the room and by that time all my furniture was upside down. So I waited on the doorstep again until my husband came home from work and, well – we didn't say nothing about it to anybody. We just cleaned up the mess.

So then, Tuesday, nothing happened strange at all. But it was on the Wednesday, my little girl was in nursery school, so it was about five to three, my mother was out in my room so I said to her 'Oh, I'd better go if I'm going to catch the bus'. So she said, 'All right I'll get the knitting from my room and come back here with the baby'. 'All right', I said. So I went to get the bus for school and when I came back my mother was on the doorstep. So I asked her what was the matter and she said the same things had happened again – that all my furniture was upside down. So we both went in to have a look, so I could see that my room was in the same kind of a mess.

So we went up the back kitchen to see if anything had been touched up there. Well that was all right: nothing had been touched.

So we went back, we went upstairs then to see if anything had been touched upstairs, and upstairs was all right. So I said, 'Come on, we'll wait on the doorstep for my husband to come home again'. So we waited. We didn't hear no sound of anything at all. So when he came home I said that my room was in the same kind of mess. And then we went up to the kitchen – and my gas stove was all turned up and – well, we didn't hear any sound of anything at all.

Then we went upstairs to go to see if the bedrooms were all right and we couldn't open the bedroom door. So my husband says that he thinks we had better call the police. 'No!' I told him. I was crying and then I said that we'd better not call the police because we couldn't tell them that our furniture was flying about by itself.

So well, anyway, we called the police and the police had to force the bedroom door open to get in and my big double bed was on top of the baby's cot behind the door. Well, he always used to go to bed in the afternoon ; I don't know why I didn't put him there then: if he had been in it, he would have been killed . . . Well, we didn't stay any longer. We went straight out after the police had been and we didn't go back until the next day to get a couple of things to wear – and all my furniture was soaking wet . . . We didn't stop another night in the house.

If we take a preliminary canter round the Rhondda Street covert we may not view the fox but at least we can start a few hares. Let us begin by supposing that Mrs Howells was not telling the truth: nobody was there to see the bottles fly at her, for instance ; we have only her word that this is what happened. Her story that her furniture was turned upside down on the first occasion is confirmed by her mother ; on the second occasion her mother called attention to the disorder and Mrs Howells confirmed it. Our conclusion must therefore be that either both were lying in conspiracy or both were telling the truth. Since each woman was present on one occasion when furniture was allegedly turned over, we are at liberty to believe that each in turn upset it and then called the husband to witness the damage on his return home: or we can include the husband in a conspiracy from the start. But we have to admit that there was one occasion when the furniture in Mrs Howells' bedroom in Rhondda Street actually was violently disturbed – no matter how or why or by whom – and that the police confirmed the disturbance. I rule out any possibility that the police could be party to a conspiracy here and accept that the double bed was found over the baby's cot and jamming the bedroom door.

It is conceivable that one or other of the women could have had a motive for creating the disturbance; it is not impossible that even one of them would have the strength to raise up a double bed and, having pulled the baby's cot under it, somehow vacate the bedroom and induce the bed to fall on the closing door and jam it. I say it is not impossible: but in my opinion extremely unlikely.

Could a third party, someone outside the Howells' household, have been able to cause the rumpus ? It may be suspicious, for instance, that Mrs Howells found the street door open after both she and her husband had shut and locked it. An intruder, maybe ? But if we blame an intruder, how do we explain away the flying milk bottles and the choking feeling experienced by both Mr and Mrs Howells? And what do we make of the bedroom door which the police had to force from the outside ? Had the intruder performed the conjuring trick of jamming the door from the inside as he left ? For his only other exit was the bedroom window and, at the time, Mrs Howells and her mother were outside the front of the house and must have seen anyone leave.

Young Mrs Marcia Howells struck me as a truthful, sincere and worried witness. I find myself in agreement with Dr Owen who said of this case 'I don't think that there was any trickery there'.[1]

One unusual feature about the Rhondda Street poltergeist is the absence of noise and bumps. Mrs Howells herself said 'We didn't hear no sound of anything at all'. This is extraordinary on two counts: first, noise and poltergeist manifestations go together like bread and butter; and secondly anyone who has tried to upset a double bed or even more so, a gas stove, will find the *lack* of noise extremely puzzling. Power to move beds and gas stoves is approaching the limit of a single adult person's muscle ; to move them without making a sound may well be beyond it.

We can conclude this introductory treatment of Mrs Howells' poltergeist by asking and trying to answer a question. What was the purpose of all this activity whether fake or genuine ? It was all directed at Mr and Mrs. Howells. It began three days after they moved into Mrs Howells' mother's house. Was its purpose to shift the family out again ? If so, it succeeded, for eventually the struggle became too much for Marcia and she, her husband and two children moved out.

Further discussion will be better left until we have examined our other two case histories, those of the Northfleet and Sauchie poltergeists.

The Northfleet house is a fairly modern council house built about thirty years ago, seemingly normal and not the kind to be haunted. Eventually though, spooks so upset the various tenants that at last the house became empty. In 1966 it was arranged that Dr George Owen would sit there all night with lights and a BBC camera crew in the hope that poltergeist phenomena might manifest themselves. The hope was not a strong one, because it now seems certain that in order to appear, such phenomena need a human focus and the house for that night would hold strangers with no previous connection with reported goings-on.

Dr Owen began his piece to camera in a bedroom by saying:

[1] BBC transmission as before.

Here I am alone at dead of night in a deserted house. Fully furnished, the property is in excellent condition yet the people are gone. Why is this ? ... About four years ago a young couple, Mr and Mrs Maxted, moved in and before long they found something amiss. Their children complained that at night there was a scratching under their bed, that the bed clothes were twitched and tweaked away from them and that they were poked and pulled while sleeping in their beds.

Here was traditional poltergeist phenomena indeed ; we could well have been 300 years back with Squire Mompesson and his children at Tidworth on Salisbury Plain.

When the Maxteds were in their sitting room below the children's bedroom they would often hear the sound of footsteps going across the bedroom floor although at the time they knew the chamber was empty. Another thing which disturbed them was the fact that little ornaments and small household articles would mysteriously disappear – sometimes for good ; at other times they would just as mysteriously turn up again tucked away in a drawer or some other hiding place.

This was not all. From time to time the house would be filled with a strange kind of smell, an unpleasant chemical smell, which would come without any seeming cause and with no explanation that they could find. Despite all their troubles and puzzlement the Maxteds stuck it out until finally Mrs Maxted saw a strange apparition. It was February 1965 about 2 o'clock in the morning. Mrs Maxted had just got back into her own bed after attending to her baby. Mr Maxted was awakened by his wife calling out 'Linda!' (the name of their older child) and was amazed to see his wife sitting up in bed with her face 'frozen into a mask of intense fear'. He was shocked too, to hear her begin to scream with terror and then to collapse by his side. Eventually she told him how she had returned from attending to the baby and had hardly got back into their bed again when she saw the figure of a little girl about six years old with fair hair come into the room. Linda is in fact red-haired, but because the height of the figure corresponded to Linda's, Mrs

35

Maxted at first thought the apparition was her own daughter. However, as the figure came towards her a terrifying change took place in it. It grew in height until it became a tall figure bending over her. She saw its face in profile and sat up screaming at the uncanny sight.

After this, not unnaturally, the Maxteds thought that enough was enough and they moved out the very next day. They were followed as tenants by Mr and Mrs Eric Essex. Eric Essex worked as a tugboat engineer and was well-used to the rough and tumble of a tough river life. He was twenty-five at the time and his wife Margaret was twenty-two. The Essex's too were persecuted. They would sit in the living room and hear footsteps overhead in the bedroom ; but in addition they heard a new noise, a sound as if the bedroom furniture was being moved – slid over the floor. Still, on inspection nothing was found out of place. Mr and Mrs Essex (like the Maxteds) reported a strange smell seeping through the house, but they described it as being the smell of something old, rotten, musty. They stuck it out for a year and a half until the happenings reached a climax quite as dramatic and strange as the earlier one with Mr and Mrs Maxted.

One night Eric Essex awoke with a whistling in his ear and at the same time realised that his bed was vibrating. It was being heaved up at one end but no human being was in sight to do it. And then to his astonishment and his considerable fear and excitement, the weirdest of phantoms formed itself at his bedside. It was glowing with a pinkish orange colour. At the edges it was rather transparent, near its centre its substance seemed more solid. Strangest of all, it was in the shape of a woman with no head. The Essex family moved out the next day.

All subjective ? All in the mind, Master Shallow ? We should be shallow ourselves to accept this explanation without further probing.

So far, apart from the apparitions, the happenings appear to have followed a mainly poltergeist pattern, but now comes something different. Next door lived a Mr and Mrs Harrison. Because of the curious interlocking way in which these particular houses are built, one of the Harrisons' bedrooms is actually above the entrance hall of the house next door. Mr and Mrs Harrison slept in this bedroom. Mrs Harrison stated that after the Essex family left and *their house was empty*, she and her husband had gone to bed one night but around about 3 am she was awakened by a noise which appeared to be coming from the hall below. In fact Mrs Harrison heard three different kinds of noise – thumping as though a child's ball was bouncing down the stairs of the house next door; then a 'honking' noise, all round her own bed; and finally a 'scratching noise'. These are her own words:

> We heard a terriffic row in there and it sort of seemed as if it came from the stairs and it was like a scratching noise and it sort of seemed as if it come from in our hallway up through into the bedroom and it was sort of like as if it was under my bed – and then I wasn't imagining it: I was awake! It sort of shot up into the bedroom where I was and it was like a scratchy noise under the bed . . . as if it was bumping up the bed, you know. It wasn't just in one part of the bed. It was all over underneath . . . It frightened me that much I had to wake my husband up. He'd stirred when the noise was there, but he didn't wake up. Anyway, I woke him and put the light on because he said to me, 'Don't be silly! Put the light off! You'll wake the children up.' Anyway, I wouldn't have the light off; I had it on. The next day I said to him that I wouldn't stop in there. I said I'd go and sleep to my mother's . . . and I said to him I'd take the children up. So he said 'Well if you like,' he said, 'you can go up for a couple of days to get it off your mind'. It frightened me that much that I didn't hardly have no sleep for about six nights!

While Mrs Harrison's description of bedtime noises and the movement of the bed fit well into the traditional poltergeist pattern, there are a number of odd things about the spook in the Northfleet house. First, the hauntings passed from one tenant to a second and even to a third neighbour. Was therefore the house the focus and not primarily the person? Secondly, are

we to assume that the haunting continued *in vacuo* even after
the tenants had left ?[1] Or thirdly, are we to believe that for
want of a human trigger the poltergeist manifestations did in
fact move to the Harrisons next door ?

I do not want to pursue these enquiries until later but I may
mention a matter connected with this house of a kind which
from time immemorial has been offered as a reason why houses
might be haunted. A Mrs Hickford, formerly Mrs Sedge, née
Clark had three sisters. The eldest, Mary Jane Clark, married
Herbert John Bennett. Mary Jane was strangled with a bootlace
on Yarmouth beach 22 September 1900, a crime for which her
husband was tried at the Old Bailey. At the time of the murder,
Herbert Bennett was courting a girl named Alice Meadows who
did not know he was married. Although defended by the celebrated British barrister Marshall Hall, Bennett was found
guilty and hanged. The youngest of the four Clark sisters was
born after Mary Jane had been murdered and was also
christened Mary Jane. The second Mary Jane died at the age
of six and a half years. Mrs Hickford, another of the four sisters,
lived for a time at the house in Northfleet.

I now pass on to the third poltergeist case treated in our film,
that of Virginia Campbell. Dr Owen, who investigated this case,
has given a meticulous and model account in his book.[2] I shall
therefore confine myself to the one eyewitness we ourselves
used in the film, covering the whole of his filmed statement
which was too long to be used in its entirety in our programme.

Virginia Campbell was at the time eleven years old and the
youngest daughter of James and Annie Campbell, citizens of
the Irish Republic living on a croft near Moville, Co. Donegal.

[1]It is suggestive that during the Christmas holiday of 1965 when the Essex's
were tenants but absent for a few days over the holiday period, the people
living nearbye at that time heard loud bangs as though doors were repeatedly being slammed and when these same near neighbours complained bitterly
to Eric Essex on his return were told that the house had been empty. A
man accused Mr Essex of lying and, in the words of the cockney song,
punched 'im up the froat'. The assault brought police intervention, the man
was prosecuted, convicted and fined.
[2]*Can We Explain the Poltergeist?*, 2 Chapter 5.

In the autumn of 1960 Virginia left her quiet and rather lonely life at 'the edge of the world' where her only regular companions apart from her parents had been her pet dog Toby and a little playmate called Anna. She went to live with her married brother Thomas and his wife at Sauchie in Scotland. Her father was preparing to sell his croft and move out, so Virginia's mother accompanied her to Scotland and found employment in a boarding house of the well known Dollar Academy which necessitated her 'living in' and therefore away from her daughter, albeit only five or six miles. In mid-October 1960 Virginia Campbell was enrolled at Sauchie Primary School. The main poltergeist manifestations of which she was the centre, in fact a true traditional 'focus', took place between 22 November 1960 and 1 December 1961 with a tailing off of phenomena up to 23 April 1961. The phenomena were of the two classical types (1) production of noises such as tapping, knocking, sawing, bumping and (2) the movements of objects by paranormal means. At least five responsible witnesses were prepared to swear to the objectivity of the phenomena, namely Rev. T. W. Lund (MA, BD) Minister of Sauchie Church of Scotland ; Dr W. H. Nisbet (MB, ChB) physician; Dr William Logan (MB, ChB) physician ; Mrs Sheila Logan (MB, ChB, DPH) physician and Dr Logan's wife ; and Miss Margaret Stewart, a qualified schoolmistress. Here then is Dr William Logan's eyewitness account:

Dr Logan: My first involvement with Virginia Campbell's poltergeist was on the evening of Saturday 26 November 1960. I was called to the house because of the incidents and happenings that had been taking place there during that night and, as it turned out, on (the) previous (four) nights.

When I arrived at the house (19 Park Crescent, Sauchie) the house owners (Virginia's brother Thomas and his wife) were in a state of excitement and tension and informed me that there had been loud knockings and noises, and pieces of furniture had been moved and that something odd was going on.

So I went up to see the child who was lying in bed looking fairly relaxed despite the obvious commotion that had been going on ; and I asked her to try and forget as much as possible that I was in the room beside her.

After I had been in the room for about 10 or 15 minutes I noticed that one of the pillows beside Virginia was beginning to move in a rather unusual fashion. If you can imagine Virginia lying with her head on this pillow here and another pillow beside her – now this pillow started to turn in a rotary fashion, thus: (*Dr Logan demonstrated the movement to the camera using a small cushion*). In addition, I noticed round about the same time or shortly afterwards, that there was an impression or indentation beginning to occur, as if something was either pulling from inside or pushing: but there was no obvious physical force bringing this about. I checked thoroughly that Virginia herself was in no position to bring about these odd movements, both by observation and by checking the position of her hands and feet. Furthermore, there was no other person close enough to Virginia on the pillow to bring this about. I waited for a little while and only one other phenomenon occurred and this was a puckering of the bedclothes. Now again, if you can try and imagine this piece of cloth as part of the coverlet on Virginia's bed, the bedclothes appeared to be pulled up and towards Virginia as if some force was trying to pull the coverlet to the child. But apart from that, nothing else happened on that evening.

After I came home – obviously this was a most exciting and interesting happening – I wondered if perhaps my dog, a golden retriever, would feel or sense anything out of the way. So I decided to take him with me when I called to see the child the next morning. It has been said that dogs have supersensory powers – most animals have supersensory powers and perhaps although nothing obvious might be happening near the child, the dog may react in some unusual manner.

However, when I got him to the house on the Sunday morning Virginia had just come home from Sunday School, as far as I remember, and she made a great fuss of the dog, comparing him unfavourably, I may say, to her own dog Toby who had been left in Ireland when she had left that country seven weeks previously to come and live in Scotland.

Nothing more was said, and nothing more was thought of the incident, really, until that night when, just after Virginia had gone to bed, she appeared to go into some form of trance and started shouting out in a loud, demanding, aggressive voice (which was entirely foreign to the normal nature of the child) that she wanted to have her own dog Toby brought to her at once. In addition, she also mentioned a childhood friend, Anna ; and it transpired that Anna and the dog and Virginia were inseparable companions. They played their childhood games together and spent most of their time, really their growing-up age, playing all sorts of childish games in a very small isolated Irish hamlet.

After the incident on Sunday night the knockings and noises and other manifestations appeared to increase in tempo, and this trance-like episode was repeated on the following evening, Monday, and again on the Tuesday.

On the Tuesday I happened to be there myself ... The Tuesday evening I went on a normal visit and heard for the first time knockings and tappings. In addition to this I made sure that my wife (who had been extremely sceptical about the whole incident and was inclined to treat it as a huge joke with a slightly quizzical look at my own mentality, shall we say) was *forced* – because that's the only word I can use to describe it – I insisted that she come with me.

When we arrived Virginia had been in bed for some time and we sat downstairs until we heard knockings that seemed to come from the room above us. We tiptoed upstairs and went into the room.

Virginia was lying in bed. She wasn't asleep. She appeared to be wide awake, but there was no doubt there was a loud knocking sound coming from the vicinity of her bed ... This phenomenon, together with another scratching noise ... were both present on this occasion. Both these noises were subsequently recorded (by BBC Scotland) at a later session the same week – actually, the following Thursday evening, two nights later. My wife expressed surprise and initially disbelief and stepped forward to satisfy herself that the noises were not in fact being made by the child lying on the bed. She examined her bedclothes very thoroughly. There was no sign of movement during the time the noises were on. She also made quite sure by very quickly lifting up the bedclothes that there was no movement of her hands or feet. But she couldn't really check by visual means. She then examined the wall of the room and checked that in actual fact the sound was not coming from the other side of the wall, but appeared to be in the vicinity of the bed.

After a short while we decided to go home, thinking that perhaps Virginia would settle down and go to sleep once we had left.

Just as we were going out the door a very unusual thing happened. It seemed unusual at the time – the noises . . . the knockings appeared to take on a 'character' in that they became extremely hurried and agitated as if something was trying to get us to stay in the room, or attract attention to the child in the bed . . . much louder than they had been previously.

However, we went home. And about an hour later I got a call to say that Virginia was in a trance-like state as she had been on the previous three evenings and was quite hysterical. I must say that I had made a point before I left to say that I wanted to be phoned any time of the night should anything of this most unusual nature happen. So I went out to Dollar[1] once again and found Virginia in a state of extreme tension, being very aggressive, demanding that certain people should come immediately and speak with her, and asking for her dog and her friend Anna. In fact (although I wasn't there at the time) I'm told that someone thought of handing her a

[1]On the advice of Dr Nisbet (Dr Logan's partner) Virginia had been taken to Dollar, about 5½ miles from Sauchie, on Monday 28 November to stay with a relative for a couple of nights.

teddy-bear and saying 'This is Toby'. But this was hurriedly rejected ; in fact it was thrown at the giver by Virginia, and she told them in no uncertain terms that this was not a dog but a teddy-bear and she, at least, knew the difference. This trance-like episode went on for about 20 or 30 minutes and then stopped. After about 2 or 3 minutes Virginia appeared to reawaken. She then asked for a cup of tea which was given her, and after which she fell into a normal sleep. During this period of sleep (and this has been noted by other observers) there was no sign at all of poltergeist phenomena.

My next visit to the house (*19 Park Crescent, Sauchie – Virginia having returned to her brother's home*) was two nights later on a Thursday evening when I decided to take a tape-recorder along with me in the hope that should any noises or sounds be heard I would have a record of these phenomena to satisfy myself amongst others, I suppose, that there was no form of mass-hypnosis – which had been suggested as a possible cause on these occasions. I set up the tape-recorder and left it running. After it had been going for about half an hour which is (as far as I remember) roughly the time between Virginia going to bed and the phenomena starting, the knocking noises were heard and also the sawing sounds. In addition to this, about an hour and a half after the various sounds had been going on, and I was out of the room at the time, Virginia gave a scream and shouted for her mummy. I was in the room within seconds and found that a linen chest had had its lid raised. Now this chest was almost at the opposite side of the room from Virginia and she certainly had no time to get out of bed, lift the chest and get back into bed again by the time I was out and in the room. Apart from that, there were no other phenomena that night. The pillows were thrown on the floor on one or two occasions, but there was no adult observer in the room at the time these things happened. The child settled down and went to sleep.

Now that is the end of my own personal contact with these phenomena but I have been given permission to read extracts from a diary that I suggested a close relative of the child should keep shortly after the events started. She noted down very carefully in her own words – by the way, this diary has never been published or read in any form before to the public, and she was very kind in allowing me to read extracts from it tonight. I would like to read the first description of the first night on which the phenomena started. It's dated Tuesday 22 November 1960: *At about 10.30 pm Margaret and Virginia were lying in bed. There was a noise like a ball bouncing on the floor. I looked under the beds in the room but couldn't see anything. No sooner had I left the room when it started again. Margaret and Virginia went downstairs (thinking that perhaps a mouse was under the bed) for a brush. The thing seemed to follow them down the stairs. We tried putting the two girls in the other bed. There was a loud knocking on the headboard, so we tried them in our bed in the other room, but the knocking still went on. It kept getting louder and louder. Then it was like a scraping on top of the bed. Virginia and Margaret went to sleep. The noise all stopped.* Well this as I say goes on every night and there is a description one day in the afternoon. This is 1.30 pm on Wednesday 14 December. A friend had just been visiting the house and after he left (I quote): *an apple came out of the dish three times. Virginia was in the house with Dad. He said while I was away an apple came out of the dish three times. The clock came off the cabinet and hit Virginia on the nose, settled on the chair just before I came back.* Again we read: *A piece of chocolate jumped off the sideboard, also a pencil. A brillo pad came out of the kitchen into the living room. The light went on twice. Virginia was using the (vacuum) cleaner. It went off and the rubber flew off the handle. A doll came off the chest of drawers on to the bed a few times. A flower came out of the vase at the bottom of the stairs. A chair tumbled over. There was a little knocking on the big chair. A table drawer opened. The cupboard door opened and the table kept moving. Then there was a knocking on the table Virginia gave three knocks and there was three knocks*

*back . . . At dinner the table moved again, knocking on the
cupboard door. Virginia was getting pinched on the side . . .
The top of Margaret's hot water bag was opened and there
was a little scraping. The girls got nipped in bed . . .
Virginia's leg was getting tickled . . . For the past three nights
there has been writing on the girls' faces. The bedcover
turned red. It was a green cover. There was a noise like somebody walking across the floor. Virginia's lips went bright red
three times and there was a noise like a ball bouncing.*
Incidentally, this bright red description, really, as far as I
could make out, what she really intended to express was that
Virginia's lips appeared to *glow* bright red – this she saw
herself. All these things and many others of a similar nature
happened right up to the final entry on 23 April 1961. It was
a Sunday and she says here – *There was a knocking on the
cupboard door.*

My own feeling about this unusual series of events is that
the child when she first came to this country was not
emotionally upset. This I discovered later and I thought to be
extremely strange, because it would seem a normal thing for
a child taken from a small isolated community to show some
signs of distress or tears: but there was no sign of this at
all. She arrived in this country and appeared to settle down in
a quiet, normal, shy manner. This too is strange, because I
felt this was abnormal, and I feel that as a result of this
abnormal suppression of instinctive and normal emotional
behaviour, some form of suppression was built up within her
subconscious. Now this was shown to me, I feel, because when
she saw the dog it sparked off a train of thought which subsequently exploded into a series of near hysterical trances in
which she demanded a return to the life that she had been
leading in Ireland before she came to this country. Now, a
child can find it very difficult, I think, in a strange land to
express itself, so her subconscious in some way or other has
hit upon this method of attracting attention to the upset
which had occurred in her normal pattern of life. And this
suppression has taken the form of poltergeist activity, in that

45

it always occurred in the vicinity of Virginia. The events were so bizarre that they were bound to attract attention of even the most casual of observers in the room or in her vicinity ; and as a result of this attention events transpired that her dog actually – as far as I remember, I think this is true – was brought over from Ireland. She was reunited with this living contact of her childhood past, and eventually she settled down and grew up a normal healthy girl.

Before I discuss Dr Logan's theory or indeed any of the general questions raised by these three actual and fairly recent poltergeist outbreaks, I want to add one or two other well-attested phenomena connected with Virginia Campbell and then to attempt a formal tabulation of the manifestations in the three cases.

The Rev T. W. Lund heard knocking coming from Virginia's bed head and felt the headboard vibrating all without a perceptible physical cause. He saw a large chest 27ft by 17ft by 14ft full of bed linen in Virginia's bedroom rock, raise itself slightly, travel eighteen inches over the linoleum and move back to its original position – again with no apparent outside help. He saw Virginia's pillow rotated horizontally through 60 degrees.

Miss Margaret Stewart, schoolmistress at Sauchie Primary School, saw Virginia trying to force her desk lid down with the lid rising of its own accord. She saw a child's desk, temporarily unoccupied, in front of Virginia rise slowly about an inch off the floor with nobody moving it. She saw a blackboard pointer on her own desk, with Virginia standing by, begin to vibrate and eventually roll off the desk. She put her hand on the desk and found it vibrating. In fact the desk itself twisted away from her.

In cases of poltergeist phenomena we frequently find witnesses of good standing, like Miss Stewart, who are the *sole* observers of phenomena. For instance, Miss Stewart was the sole outside observer of the levitation of the child's desk and the movement of the blackboard pointer. In such cases, I believe we ought to apply what I call the 'safety in numbers' rule. In other words, where similar phenomena are observed in the same or other poltergeist hauntings by other observers, we can accept the evidence except where there are obvious reasons mitigating against the acceptance. I believe that both the Rev Lund and Miss Stewart did see objectively what they claimed to have seen.

It will be useful now to summarise the kind of phenomena observed with the Marcia Howells, the Northfleet house and Virginia Campbell poltergeists.

(1) Two of the examples demonstrated *noises* of various kinds and intensities, sometimes very loud; one (Marcia Howells) was mysterious for its complete lack of noise.

(2) All three demonstrated *movement of objects* without perceptible physical cause, and in two cases actual levitation (Marcia Howell's milk bottles, Miss Stewart's school desk, Mr Lund's linen chest).

(3) *Pinchings, pullings and ticklings or other forms of attack* on the principals took place in all three cases.

These three types of phenomena are amply attested by reputable witnesses. There are two other types of phenomena which take rather more swallowing but which may gain evidence from the 'safety in numbers' rule when grouped with similar phenomena to be mentioned in future chapters. I refer to:

(4) *Apparitions* which occurred at the Northfleet house as attested by Mrs Maxted and Mr Essex. We have no indication as to whether the apparition, if objective, was one and the same.

(5) *Stigmata*. In Virginia Campbell's haunting we hear of three nights when 'there has been writing on the girls' faces' (diary quoted by Dr Logan); and 'Virginia's lips went bright red three times' (diary).

While I feel that little can be gained until a later chapter from discussing the apparitions, it may be worth while to talk about the stigmata. I think we should be wrong to dismiss the writing on the girls' faces out of hand as the mischief of two little minxes (Margaret was Virginia's niece though both were children) who had decided to augment the phenomena with marks made by finger nails or even lipstick: at no time and by no witnesses is there even any suggestion that Virginia was normally (as opposed to paranormally) responsible for any of the phenomena. Because of my own experience in a case subsequently to be discussed (Chapter V) I accept the genuineness of the writing and the glowing lips: in the classical stigmata cases, which appear to occur particularly among religious enthusiasts, it seems logical to believe that each person is responsible for his own stigmata. Virginia's case is puzzling because while one could accept her, as the poltergeist 'focus', being responsible for her own stigmata – who was responsible for Margaret's ?

The question which ended the last section leads us naturally to a discussion of what is a poltergeist ? The traditional view was that there did exist mischievous, even malevolent spirits who tormented their victims with phenomena such as I have been describing.

The mention of 'their victims' gives us a clue from which to begin our own detective work. For from the earliest recorded cases there always was a victim, an actual person, who suffered. This at least is sure ground, a poltergeist has to have a 'focus'.

In the past it has been commonly believed that the focus was usually a little girl at a pre-puberty stage of physical development or entering puberty. Later studies have shown that boys as well as girls can be poltergeist foci and that while the age limits of most known subjects range from thirteen to eighteen years, there have been both males and females ranging in age from ten years to twenty-seven[1]. In the next two chapters I shall discuss a very complicated case of haunting where (if I am right) some of the phenomena were of poltergeist origin and the focus in question was an adult male of thirty-three. What

---

[1]George Owen gives a ratio of 2:1 in favour of girls being affected by poltergeist phenomena: *Can We Explain the Poltergeist?*, p. 368.

appears to be a common factor to all foci is that during the time of the persistence of the phenomena the victims are suffering strong emotional disturbance and possible physical change ; and a further common factor is that the phenomena cease when the victims are asleep.

It has struck students that the cessation of poltergeist phenomena when the focus is asleep is a fact of paramount importance. But since science still appears to be a long way off understanding the biological function of sleep, we are perhaps not that much further forward. What I do believe is that we can make two broad claims (1) the cessation of phenomena when the focus is asleep is perhaps the strongest proof of the axiom that poltergeist phenomena *are* caused by the victim, (2) the part of the victim responsible for triggering the phenomena is that part of his make-up which is temporarily dormant during sleep.

Now, the part of the brain which is out of normal action during sleep is the cortex, and the status of the sleeping person is that he is unaware of his normal surroundings, he is unconscious. And here there may appear to be a contradiction, for while the focus has to be conscious to produce poltergeist phenomena, it is universally agreed that the foci are unaware of their connection with the phenomena (until told – and even then find the fact difficult to believe) and certainly are not aware of how they produce the effects – nor, I might say, is anybody else. But I suggest that the contradiction is only apparent: the cortex has to be active during the production of phenomena, but the actual seat of production I take to be another part of the brain, and that part *the one of whose functions we are never conscious whether waking or sleeping*: 'which of you by taking thought can add one cubit to his stature ?' This Secret Service section of the brain is that which among other things regulates a person's bodily functions, keeps his heart beating, his lungs pumping, his digestion stirring and, when malfunctioning, produces bodily and mental disorders.

There may be another clue to help answer the question, what is a poltergeist ? in what appears to be a fact, namely that Man is unique in being able to produce poltergeist phenomena. Animals do not have poltergeists.

What difference is it then in Man, which allows certain individuals willy-nilly to produce poltergeist phenomena: Man is not different from living animals to a degree which would make him unique as far as his anatomy or physiology is concerned. He is placed in a class by himself on account of one thing – his central nervous system.

It would be egregious of me, a layman, to attempt to discuss in detail so complicated a subject as man's central nervous system. This is a field for a specialist. I must content myself with asking questions rather than with issuing statements. But first, I may be permitted to clear a bit of ground to show the wood from the trees. We all know that the central nervous system contains the brain and the spinal cord: we know that the three main divisions of the brain are the brain stem, the cerebellum, and the cerebral hemispheres. The oldest part of the brain from an evolutionary point of view is the *brain stem ;* the newest part is that which covers the cerebral hemispheres – the *cortex* – and it is this part which during evolution has so burgeoned in Man and has grown comparatively little in animals, even those nearest to Man, the apes.

A concomitant of the growth of Man's cortex has been the flowering of his *psyche* – taken for my purpose as a layman to mean the sum total of Man's sensations, emotions, drives and thoughts. The psyche is literally *the* brain-child, it is a function of the brain which gave it birth. But to change the metaphor, the psyche appears to be in continual reaction with the brain and we have what radio sound engineers call *feed-back.* In radiophonics feed-back produces disturbance, howling, cacophony. The ultimate reaction of the disturbed psyche with the brain is suicide or should we say matricide ? – when the brain-child terminates the life of the parent which produced it. But long before that 'final solution' is reached, the psyche which is disturbed may have forced the brain to produce effects which psychiatrists recognise as hysteria, melancholia, anxiety, any kind of psychosomatic illness and indeed, physical changes in outward appearance including stigmata.

If therefore, I may crudely summarise my argument so far: I believe that, on the evidence, we may claim as a working hypothesis that poltergeist phenomena are produced unconsciously by an individual whose psyche is disturbed, that the disturbed psyche reacts on the oldest part of the brain, the brain stem, which by means unknown to science produces the commonly recognisable poltergeist phenomena. And these phenomena are the overt cry for help: as the poem says (if we can put the words into the mouth of the poltergeist focus) 'I was . . . not waving but drowning'[1].

Just how the phenomena are produced nobody knows. Dr George Owen believes that 'the magnitude of the mechanical actions of the poltergeist is never much different from that which adult man could achieve with his own unaided strength'[2] I hesitate to disagree with a man of Dr Owen's scholarship and experience, but I do: faced with personal experience of poltergeist phenomena to be discussed in the next two chapters, I got the feeling that terrific and terrifying power was on call. In fact, Dr Owen is himself willing to keep an open mind, and I feel much more in sympathy with the sentiments with which he concludes his superb study:

It is plausible to suppose that the forces potentially present are comparable in magnitude with normal biological ones. But this we do not know, and indeed, as within the atom, titanic energies may be latent for exploitation. And should this be so, it may be best for them to remain a riddle enwrapped in a mystery until such time as Man's sociological genius (if such he has) shall elevate him from his present rank of sorcerer's apprentice.[3]

[1]Stevie Smith 'Not waving but drowning' pub. Andre Deutsch 1957.
[2]*Can We Explain the Poltergeist?* p. 362.
[3]Ibid, p. 436.

4
A Mild Case
of Haunting

The case I shall recount now is a baffling one. I found it also exciting, terrifying at times, puzzling and illuminating by turns, and a startling mixture of practically every kind of psychic manifestation you can think of, including ectoplasm. This statement is, I know, calculated to bring discredit on the phenomena right at the start and to call up Victorian frauds with butter-muslin, illuminated paint and trumpets on strings ; in fact, after we had transmitted a film on this haunting, a doctor who had seen it wrote to me and said (among other things) 'England is peculiar in the widespread belief in hauntings and supernatural influences, and may thus be regarded as in some ways intellectually backward . . . It is about time this nonsense is discredited before another generation gets enthralled by it'[1].

Intellectually backward ? Nonsense ? The reader must judge. I only say that I was myself present when many of the phenomena took place and that I was continually on the look-out for fraud, having come a long way since the early days when I was largely on the watch for broadcasting programme material: during the whole pursuit of this case I was never prepared to believe in what people commonly call the super-natural, and I still do not believe in it, although some of the things I saw and heard were indeed beyond belief.

The people who were central to the phenomena described in

[1]Letter to the author from Dr Keith Thompson MB, ChB, DRCOG, MRCGP.

this and the next chapter are still alive, except one[1], for which reason I have referred to some of them by their Christian names only.

It all began for me one day in the early summer of 1965 when my colleague Bob Saunders returned to my office at the BBC Television Film Studios after an errand to a local photographer who had set up business in former Church rooms known as Buckell Hall. This photographer, thirty-three years old, Christian name George, a big, hefty fellow with the physique of a rugby forward and weighing seventeen stone, had moved into the hall about two years previously. His business was beginning to flourish and frequently he did still photographs for use in my Travel and Exploration Unit. Bob Saunders had been to collect a batch of stills, and when he got back said to me, 'There's something funny going on over there at Buckell Hall'.

'How do you mean, funny?'

'George says the place is haunted.'

There was silence for a second in my office, then Anne Whillock my secretary, Saunders and I all burst out laughing. But it was obvious from what Bob Saunders told us that it was no laughing matter for George, his blonde assistant Rita, and another part-time assistant, Ann, who was Rita's cousin. Not to put too fine a point on it, the girls were very frightened. George himself was upset because it seemed as though what was happening was designed to force his workers to leave, make him vacate the hall and so destroy his photographic business.

Because Buckell Hall was only ten minutes walk away from the film studios it seemed (if it really was haunted) an ideal location to which we could take cameras and recorders quickly. The temptation to film a ghost or a poltergeist at work was too great for me and within half an hour I was walking back with Saunders to question George and case the joint. What I was told by three different people who had witnessed phenomena decided me to continue – but cautiously.

[1]George Medhurst, a Council Member of the British Society for Psychical Research who died tragically in 1971.

For some years I had known Dr Eric Dingwall, an investigator of psychic phenomena with a world-wide reputation – perhaps best remembered with Trevor Hall as the demolisher of the reputation of Borley Rectory, claimed by Harry Price to be 'the most haunted house in England.' I reckoned that if 'Ding' would go over Buckell Hall and its occupants and pronounce that there was something worth investigating, then that would constitute a go-ahead for me.

On 13 July 1965 Dr Dingwall came up from his home near Battle in Sussex and spent three hours questioning George and Rita and examining Buckell Hall for cracks, subsidence, underground streams or anything which might be responsible for strange noises and movements. After making the introduction to George, I did not myself stay, but left Bob Saunders to make a complete tape-recording of what transpired. It is from this recording that I shall soon quote. When Dingwall and Saunders came back to my office, I looked at Ding and said, 'Well. Is it a fraud or not ?'

Dingwall returned my gaze with his bright blue, piercing eyes and said 'I don't think so. The photography effects are puzzling. I don't like them. I can't think they can be psychic. Photography is so crammed full of these snags. But as to the other effects – I would call it a mild case of haunting.'

Dr Dingwall had based his opinion on having found no structural defect in the hall and on the statements of two main witnesses, George and Rita. Samples of the haunting phenomena follow, being quoted from the transcription of the recording made while Dingwall examined the hall.

George and a male assistant, Jimmy, together with Rita were one night engaged in photography which entailed periods of working in complete darkness or at times with a single, shaded bulb. During one of the dark periods Rita believed she was attacked. At first, she seems to have thought it was a practical joke played on her by one of the two men, but when she discovered they were twenty feet away from her she became frightened:

Rita: It felt as though something was pressing on my neck just there, and then somebody blew – literally blew down my neck – it was too long for a puff of wind because up until this point I had worked everything out to logic. You see, everything that had gone wrong till this period had a logical explanation. Then this thing blew down my neck – when I turned round like this and George wasn't there, I suddenly realised this thing was attacking me. And thereupon I had hysterics![1]

On another occasion Ann, Rita's cousin, was helping out. She had been told of the odd occurrences and without having experienced them herself would not believe:

George: We were working in the studio there and then suddenly at about – what was it ? nine or half past nine ? – we heard without any shadow of doubt – and not outside the building, but *inside* – we heard footsteps walk down behind the flat (*a high partition of wood and canvas used for moveable scenery*). And I was able, while the footsteps were walking, to say to Ann 'Now, watch what comes out the other side!' And Ann was able to watch like this – and *nothing*! And I said, 'Now come with me round the back of the flat – did you hear that ?' She said, 'Yes! – I'd swear it on the Bible!' We looked behind the flat – nothing there.

George described another happening for which he could not account.

George: We have had circumstances in the studio and in the room (the darkroom) where suddenly the temperature drops to a point where you are so

[1]This and the following quotations are taken from Dr Dingwall's interrogation at Buckell Hall on 13 July 1965.

55

cold that you get goose-pimples and you shiver. Now, we can now think that this may be a draught, a thermal, a current of air, somebody passing – but it is so *local* that you are able to step into it and out of it. And the temperature change between stepping in and out is as much as when you'd say, 'Well; you'll catch pneumonia!' It's like stepping into a meat safe and coming out of a meat safe into the hot sunshine and going back into a meat safe. But it is so small an area that you can study and put your hands up . . .

Now after these cold patches that we'd had and after hearing these footsteps walking down behind, we – Ann, Rita and Jimmy – not myself, could smell what they thought was a thick perfume, like sort of an incense – *they* could smell this, I couldn't smell it.

Rita: It started off – I was sort of further up the studio than the other two, and it gradually worked up and I thought 'Golly! that's a funny smell,' and it gradually drifted down and it left me and gradually went on –

George: But I smelt nothing.

Dingwall: Were you in the line of where it was drifting?

George: Yes, but I couldn't smell it. Now I smelt nothing, but about five minutes later – I was working a camera – I leapt out of my seat feeling that somebody'd burnt me with a cigarette in the back. Now it just for all the world felt as if someone who smoked had stood there like this and put their cigarette against my back. And I jumped – didn't I? – I literally jumped out of my chair. I swore somebody'd burnt me there. And of course, there was nobody behind me . . . Jimmy and I had to work here very late nights, till 2 o'clock and 3 o'clock. Now, I'm not frightened of the dark. I'm not worried about it . . . But it got to the point where we were both working here together just to keep one another company. It got to a point where we were out there together, we would feel a cold draught together and once we got this cold period, then our photography would start to go haywire.

Dingwall: Did you notice any connection? Are you hinting there was a connection?

George: Oh definitely, oh definitely, yes! ... Sometimes, I must inject here, that when we've had these cold patches and things, we could look up in the roof and our roof lights were swinging – quite deliberately you know – not slight but deliberate ... On another occasion we did the cookery book for GEC which was quite a gigantic job. We had to get the food down here and such, and it had to be laid out and we had to cook and reshoot until we got it absolutely perfect ... We laid out the food on a blue background piece of paper measuring 9ft wide and probably 5ft from back to front on a huge table. It took us roughly an hour and a half to two hours, I should think, to get the food laid out just as we wanted it. We were about to shoot the picture and although this sounds quite ridiculous – but the women[1] that were here will tell you this – it started raining large drops of water all over the blue background ... But it didn't rain on anything other than the blue background. You could stand on the outside of it, couldn't you? and no spots of water came down. But the background was so spotted with water that all the food was shifted off again ... Now the next thing that we had happening here, we had a 'phone call from the

[1]Miss Margaret Leader and Miss E. Brumstead working for GEC (Domestic Equipment) Ltd, Hanger Lane, Ealing W5. In a letter dated 17 September 1965 these two ladies confirmed that 'the table was being covered with blue paper and just as it was put on the table water marks appeared on it.' In the same letter they mention having seen lights dim and go on and off unaccountably and 'some large pieces of scenery falling'.

57

police one night about – Oh, it must have been about half-past twelve. Two young policemen had 'phoned and said that they had found the front door swinging open and they had made their way into the hall here to protect the property. They came and sat in here (*the office*) and looked for an address or telephone number and managed to phone me. And they said 'Are we glad you've come to lock this place up!' And I said 'Why ?' At the time we'd had some hard-board in the hall: they said, 'Well, we were sitting here and suddenly there was an almighty sort of rustling noise out there (*in the studio*) and all the hardboard in the hall and all the back-grounds that were standing there fell over on the floor. It took us by surprise,' and being police-men you'd have thought they'd have investigated, but instead they shot straight out into the street and lit a cigarette and sort of worked out who was coming back first ... Since that time we've been very, very careful, very careful indeed, to ensure that the front door is in fact locked.

Dingwall: It hasn't become unlocked since ?

Rita: Yes!

George: Yes – that door's been found open by the police four times.

Because of the odd happenings and now police intervention, George decided to seek help from the police. It was agreed that Rita should visit Ealing Police Station and ask if there was any history to this place. She had no luck, but, George continues:

about a week later two sergeants came round here in their uniforms and said, 'We have come from the Police Station regarding the enquiry made by the lady ...' – I must go back a little: I came here one night after the door had been found open – I decided I would come back and make a double check in the evenings ... and standing outside the door as clear as I can see you now was a policeman, very young, with a dent in his forehead as if he'd had, probably, a motor cycle accident or had a trepanning operation. Anyway, he had a ginger beard and ginger hair and this was as clear and as solid as you, I'm sure. I just caught him turning into the door and I said, 'Can I help you?' He said, 'I'm just checking to make sure the door's secure as I believe you have found this door open on several occasions.' And I said, 'Yes, we have.' I said, 'I don't know how it keeps coming open, but it seems to open on its own.' 'Ha! Ha!' he said. I said, 'You laugh, but do you know anything about this?' 'I could tell you a lot about this place, sir,' so I said, 'Really? What?' So he said, 'Quite frankly, sir, I haven't got the time, but I could tell you a lot.' So I thought, 'Well, he's very interested – he knows a lot about this place, he's the person we should see.' So when Rita said she would go to the Police Station, I said 'Well, if you are going, ask for the policeman with the ginger beard because he obviously knows the place, he's lived here and probably knows it from a child.' When she asked for him they told her there was no such policeman – he doesn't exist. There's only two with a beard that they know of, and neither of those are ginger ....

Rita: They hadn't anybody with a dent in his head as well.

George: These two sergeants said 'There is a policeman here (*in Ealing*) that can remember way back – an elderly policeman ... and he said that he remembers this hall because there was a child murdered here – and he remembers taking a

> pram from this actual hall to the courthouse to
> use it in evidence, and that the man himself was
> subsequently hung and his wife jailed ...
>
> *Dingwall*: Did they give you a date ?
> *Rita*: 1941-2[1].

There was at least one event which George did not mention
to Dr Dingwall. His reasons for not doing so were probably
complicated: he no doubt felt that the event was so outlandish
as to be unbelievable, in which case the listener must surely
suspect that his informant was either lying, had had an hallucin-
ation or was going off his head. When George got to know Bob
Saunders and me better, he told us of the happening.

He was alone in the large studio one night when he saw an
oilcan take flight from a ledge along one wall just above head
height and move horizontally through the air for fifteen or
twenty feet and then fall vertically to the floor. This is how he
described it in his own words:

> I was working here late one night and I just happened to
> look up into the roof and I saw that one of our lamps was
> starting to swing. In several seconds the lamps over to the
> right started to swing and gradually they all started to swing
> in the same circular motion at about the same speed. I
> walked to the end of the studio, thinking maybe that it was a
> draught that had suddenly come through – any excuse again
> – and I happened to look at the far end of the studio – to this
> end, and I couldn't believe my eyes. I saw an oilcan from
> over there on the shelf literally float through the air, in slow
> motion, as if something or someone was holding it. It must
> have travelled at least fifteen to twenty feet in absolute slow
> motion, perfect movement. And suddenly it crashed to the
> floor[2].

George could not, as he says, believe his eyes. And yet the
event had happened. Had he known it, he was of course in good
company – Marcia Howells, for instance, with her bottles;

[1]For a discussion of this incident see below page 70ff.
[2]BBC TV Programme, *Two Steps in the Dark*.

Virginia Campbell with her apples, clock and Brillo soap pad ; and (to quote but one other) Henry Durbin, that highly respected citizen of Bristol whom I mentioned on page 25 and who wrote of an incident in 1762:

> On the chest of drawers (*at the 'Lamb' Inn*) stood a wineglass which I saw glitter in the sun, and was astonished to see it rise from the drawers without hands. It rose gradually about a foot perpendicularly from the drawers ; then the glass seemed to stand, and thereupon declined backwards, as if a hand had held it ; it was then flung with violence about five feet, and struck the nurse on the hip a hard blow. There was no person near the drawers when it rose ; the children (*Molly and Dobby Giles, daughters of the licensee of the 'Lamb' inn*) were standing near me, who saw it and ran to the other end of the room, fearing that it would be flung at them, as things generally were ... This was about nine in the morning (*5 January 1762*) in clear daylight, close by a sash-window[1].

The nurse who had been struck showed her hip next day to one of the maids at the *Lamb* : the maid affirmed that the place was bruised black and blue.

There is one very remarkable similarity between George's and Durbin's accounts. George says he saw the oil can move 'as if something or somebody was holding it.' Durbin says, 'the glass seemed to stand, and thereupon declined backwards, as if a hand had held it.' Indeed the objects which are described by George, Marcia Howells, Virginia Campbell's diarist and Durbin all have a *floating* movement through the air as though for a time they had been insulated from the force of gravity – or as if gravity had been neutralised by some equally powerful force. If there *is* another force, then it can also act very violently as is attested by both Marcia Howells with her bottles and Durbin with his wine-glass. Perhaps in the very recent past we have become more receptive to a belief in objects which move through the air in defiance of previously accepted physical laws, for we have all seen astronauts floating not only in space but in 'simulated space' on earth.

[1]Durbin, *A Narrative*.

I shall take up this subject again with additional evidence in my last chapter. But now to return to Buckell Hall. There's no doubt that the people in Buckell Hall who were subjected to the torments came to feel that a malevolent presence was centred in the darkroom and in particular over the green door in the darkroom. In his interview with Dingwall, George mentioned the feelings of two of his employees, Jim and Pam (a married woman) concerning the darkroom:

> After Pam had mentioned this to Jim ... Jim then said to me that he always felt uneasy in this room; and I likewise, now finding myself not alone with this opinion, said, 'I too feel terrible down here' ... It meant, you see, that he was holding off and so was I, because we didn't want to sort of convince one another that we were rather worried being on our own in the dark. Anyway ... I said, to Pam, 'What do you think could be down there?' And she said, 'Well, I don't know, whatever it is ... I don't say there's a ghost, but', she said, 'whatever the horrible feeling is, it hangs over your head behind you by the green door.' Now I must say at this point, this is where I would have felt it: if anybody said to me, 'Where do you feel whatever it is, is looking at you?' ... I say over there by the green door. It was at this point that I said to Jim, 'What do you feel, then?' So he said, 'Well, I don't know. It just feels as though there's something with you all the time.' And I said, 'Well, where'd you say it was, Jim?' And he said, 'Well, I'd say behind me, over by the green door.'

George went on to tell Dingwall that, after the interview with the two sergeants already mentioned, he realised that the police were unlikely to help him. As he said to Dingwall, 'I'm not really interested in what happens *as long as it goes away*. I mean, from your point of view you sort of want to foster it – from my point of view *I want to get rid of it!* Because to you this is something wonderful; to me, this is something dreadful!'

In fact, before applying to the police for assistance, George had gone to the Church. A canon (whose name he forgot) visited the hall and suggested an exorcism for which he would need to obtain his bishop's permission. George then got cold feet, for he was renting the hall from the Church Commissioners and felt that if they believed there was anything amiss, they might turn him out and the 'presence's' aim would have been achieved anyway. He dropped the exorcism idea. Then, after failure with the police he recounts, 'I thought there must be a sneaky way out of it. Well, someone said to me, the best way out of this is to get the Psychic Research people down. So again, not knowing anything about this, I decided "Yes" and so I believe Rita made contact with them.'

George plainly believed that the Society for Psychical Research was on a par with any other pest control organisation such as the borough disinfestation unit, or even the Pied Piper, and that they would rid him of his spooks.

Miss Mary Rose Barrington, a Council Member of the British Society for Psychical Research, arrived late one night at Buckell Hall for a preliminary investigation. George gave her a rundown of the happenings and mentioned how lights would either dim or go on and off unaccountably. He took her to the darkroom with the green door. George told Dingwall that Miss Barrington asked the empty air for 'some sort of sign' and at once one of the bulbs went out. Miss Barrington said, 'Of course, this could happen':

Dingwall: Did you put another bulb in when it went ? Did you try that ?

George: No we didn't. It was quite late when she arrived you see, about one o'clock in the morning. She said she'd like to see ... if whatever was there wanted a medium to come along, and would it make some other sign, and of course we had then this grey and dimming of the intensity of the lights down there, to which she shouted something like 'Oh, my God!' rushed out of the hall and left me down there ... And I flew out of the hall and shut the doors ... She did say to me outside 'I would like to bring somebody else along.'

Miss Barrington came again accompanied by another investigator, a man whose name George does not remember. The man brought with him a portable table and a red electric lamp.

Dingwall: Oh, he brought the table with him? That's good.

George: He came into the hall and sat down with the table and he said ... 'What sort of things happen?' Miss Barrington said ... 'Mr (George) said that lights go out.' So he said, 'Well, I would like to see that.' And so we turned the lights out in the studio and they put their little red light on with the table and, hey presto! their light immediately went out and the electric fire went off!

Dingwall: The fuse had gone?

George: We don't know. We just threw the fuse away and did not bother to check it ... But the thing is, on her first occasion she said she'd like to see something with the lights and, as I say, within two minutes the bulb blew. On *his* first occasion here he said, 'I understand the bulbs go' and as soon as we started this little table rapping, the lamp went out and the fire went off ... Then he said where do we normally get the main response, and we said we felt it was in the small room at the back and so we all adjourned to the (darkroom) ... We were in the back room, you see, and the table sort of rocked violently – Jimmy was there, wasn't he? Jimmy, he and myself and Rita – it rocked rather violently and we heard this knocking sound on the table and it did sort of say 'yes' and 'no' ... and then ...

Rita: There were funny reflections ...

George: He saw light or something, what he thought, on the wall ... He thought he could see a sort of light on the wall, and so he said was there a

	light? And one could see it, and one couldn't: so he said he'd investigate it. Well, I was sitting here like this whilst he moved his seat to investigate there where Rita was – and as he did so, the table shot across the room and pinned him –
Dingwall:	(interrupting) Oh! Lovely!
George:	... pinned him against the bench at the far end. But, I mean, it went with such suddenness. If anybody had pushed it, it would have been me because Miss Barrington would have had to push this way. Jimmy was sitting over at the far end –
Dingwall:	How far away was the wall on which the strange man was examining the light? How far away from the table?
Rita:	I would say the table went four to six feet ... and I wasn't pushing. I was just sitting here like this ... the table rushed across the room and left me ...
George:	So anyway, after this had happened, they went and said they would bring back a medium ... Jim said to me, 'You know – did you honestly push it?' And I said, 'No, *I* didn't push it – did *you* push it?' And he said, 'No, I had nothing to do with it – in fact, I was taken unawares.'

George's reactions to those goings-on were anything but sanguine. He began to suspect that having found himself like the fisherman with a jinn already out of the bottle, the people he had invited to help were by no means anxious to force the jinn back in but were eager to conjure out others to join him.

Some three weeks after the table incident, Miss Barrington returned with the first man and a new man, a medium. Besides George, there were also present from his party Rita, her cousin Ann and Jimmy. The SPR representatives sat side by side round the table, to which George objected; he told Dingwall, 'I didn't like this idea because, I thought, you know, it gives too much opportunity for cheating.' But the SPR people said

C*

everything would be all right as it was. However, the first message from the rocking table instructed the party to split up, which was done.

George: Anyway, he went into this so-called trance . . . He then had this voice of a Chinese gentleman – is it the 'guide' or something ? – on the 'other side'.

Dingwall: Yes, Yes.

George: And he said, 'We're here tonight!' . . . and could he help us. And the Chinese voice said that in actual fact he could see several spirits here – there was a young one and an older one, and that a lot of the things which had happened here couldn't be credited to the older one, but more to the younger one which was a restless spirit. But he said there was a man here that was walking the place who was very unhappy and he didn't want us here. He'd been on his own and he wanted to remain on his own . . . He was going to do everything he could to move us . . . So I said, 'Why is it you don't want us here ?' and . . . this Chinese voice said he was very sulky and he wouldn't talk : he wanted to be on his own. And I said there was room enough for both of us ; we weren't harming him, and why was it that we seem to get these worst occasions when we worked here late ? And . . . this thing on the other side said that it was his way of getting us to leave here, and why didn't we take our business elsewhere ? Now we hadn't told them (SPR representatives) that our business . . . was becoming inefficient through his mistakes, but he said he was going to do all he could to make sure that we left here. And we said, 'Well, we're not going to tolerate this. There's enough room for us to work together!' But (the medium) said that he has left this room now – he has gone to another room, a room at the back of the hall and he likes it there better – so could we all move – and so, of course, the medium then came out of his trance. So we all then went back to this original green room and again (the medium) went back into this sort of a trance, and he said, 'Oh yes, I can er .... you know, is he there now ?' and the Chinese voice said, 'Oh yes, he's here now. I can see him! He's standing over by the door! He's very sulky and he won't talk ...' So the Chinese chap said, 'I may get him to talk but the medium will have to go into a deeper trance.'

However, the attempt to get the entity standing by the green door to talk proved fruitless. The party broke up.

George: Well, after they'd been here we had worse trouble than we'd had when they weren't here. I phoned (Miss Barrington) and said, 'What is going to happen – we're worse off now than we were. Now, I thought you said when you came you were going to get rid of this for us ?' So she said, 'Well, I'll be honest: we don't claim to get rid of it. We just claim to make it sometimes better.' So I said, 'This means now that I'm left with something to square up ...' so she said, 'But we're interested.'

Everyone who didn't have to live with the disturbance was 'interested' and that included me. It was now over six months since the SPR representatives had been active in the case and still the phenomena continued. When Dr Dingwall indicated to me that he believed there was something worth investigating and recording if possible on tape and film, I asked George if he would co-operate with us. He agreed. However, because I was due for a sabbatical leave after twenty years service with the BBC, I had to find someone to deputise for me during the three months I should be away. I chose Bob Saunders who agreed to follow Dingwall's advice to set up a small circle of people who would sit once a week in the hall and try to establish contact with whatever it was that caused the disturbances. As a medium for any messages they would use a table. Spiritualist sittings with a table have a mixed history. When Mrs W. Hayden, an American lady, came to England in October 1852 as a professional medium, she was perhaps directly responsible for a wave of table-rapping which swept across the country in early 1853. High and low literally took a hand in this exciting and cheap Victorian parlour pastime. No doubt it was a change from sentimental ballad singing and some strong-minded people probably put it in the same category as a harmless amusement. But even though Queen Victoria and Prince Albert extracted messages from the table, there were those who attributed the raps to direct intervention by the Devil himself[1]. As seems inevitable with this kind of odd phenomena, few scientists were prepared to bring ridicule on themselves from their fellows by stooping to investigate so obvious (to them) a fraud or childish game. Those who did believe, postulated what they called an Odic force or Odylic force which was supposed to resemble electricity and magnetism: it was believed to have been revealed by the mesmeric researches of Baron K. Von Reichenbach, a gentleman whom most contemporary scientists would have found blood-brother to Baron Munchausen. The British scientist W. Faraday wrote in the *Times* of 30 June 1853 and the *Athenaeum* of 2 July 1853 of his experiments to show that table-tapping was caused neither by the beneficient Odylic force nor the malevolence of the Devil, but by the unconscious muscular action of the sitters. This explanation is one which modern Psychical Researchers, in my experience, find most acceptable. But they do not allow this to discredit the moving table ; in fact, I might encapsulate their position by borrowing a contemporary slogan and say that for them 'the medium is the message.'

[1] N. S. Godfrey, *Table Turning Tested and Proved to be the result of Satanic Agency*, London 1853 ; E. Gillson, *Table Turning, the Devil's Modern Master-Piece*, Bath 1853. For Queen Victoria's table-turning see E. Longford, *Victoria R.I.*, London 1964, p. 339.

Shortly after the meeting between the workers at Buckell Hall and Dr Dingwall, George was approached again by Miss Barrington of the Society for Psychical Research and a 'seance' was arranged to be held in the hall on 23 July at 10.30 pm. Bob Saunders phoned Miss Barrington and asked if he could attend and bring an assistant. He also sought permission to tape-record the proceedings. By this time I was on my way with my family to Norway ; so on receiving permission, Bob took with him to the seance my secretary Anne Whillock.

The SPR party consisted of Miss Barrington and George Medhurst (both council members of the British SPR) and two helpers, Benson Herbert and Manfred Casseirer. There was also a lady called Adrienne.

An attempt was made to establish contact (presumably, as far as the medium Benson Herbert was concerned 'with the other side') in the large studio. This attempt proved unsuccessful, apparently because stray light from the street upset the medium.

The party then retired to the small darkroom with the green door and a further attempt was made to establish contact in total darkness. Saunders taped the whole proceedings using two separate machines and two microphones to obtain a 'stereo' effect and also to ensure having two completely independent recordings of the session. Music was played from a small gramophone to help Benson Herbert to achieve a state of trance. The sitters had formed a circle by holding hands around a table. Manfred Casseirer then spoke in a high-pitched voice that was immediately identified by Adrienne as that of a little girl. The 'voice' said her name was Margaret and then went into incomprehensible babble.

The circle was broken and an attempt was made to contact 'Margaret' through the table. For this sitting Miss Barrington, Anne Whillock, George and Saunders dropped out and sat just behind the others.

The procedure was that questions were addressed to the table and replies were formed from raps or rockings of the table – one rap for NO, two raps for YES, and a number of raps between 1 and 26 to indicate the appropriate letter of the alphabet. According to George Medhurst the rapping or rocking could well be unconsciously manipulated by one of the sitters: 'it is not the actual physical tapping that is important, but the quite unexplainable information sometimes received in the end'.

The table on this occasion did rock, according to Saunders sometimes very violently, and the information (summarised) boiled down to: MARGARET – TWO YEARS OF AGE – MURDERED BY HER FATHER IN 1937 IN BUCKELL HALL – IS NOW WITH HER MOTHER – IS A CATHOLIC. MARGARET ASKED URGENTLY FOR A ROMAN CATHOLIC PRIEST AND PRAYERS FOR HER SOUL.

To break off for a time from the seance: that a murder ever took place in the hall is unconfirmed, but it is known that a child (and her mother) were murdered in a house immediately across a very narrow street from the hall. A statement by an officer from Ealing Police Station to Rita and George maintained that the murdered baby's pram had been kept in Buckell Hall during the period of the trial for murder of a young airman, Charles Koopman. A newspaper report of 11 September 1943 said 'Charles Koopman, 22, and his wife, Gladys Patricia Koopman, 21, appeared at Ealing today charged with the murder of Gladys Levina Brewer, 21, and her two-year-old daughter Shirley, at Grove Place, Ealing, between Wednesday night and Thursday'. The report went on to say that when the couple were charged the man replied 'no' and the woman made no response. At the inquest the woman who lived in a flat above the Brewers said that when she came home on Thursday two neighbours asked her if she had seen anything of Mrs Brewer and Shirley. When there was no answer to her knock, the neighbour said 'I opened the window of the living room, and when I pushed up the blackout I saw Mrs Brewer lolling in the armchair. She had a cushion over her face.'

When the couple came up on remand on 28 September, the *London Evening News* reported:

the case against Mrs Koopman was dismissed. Koopman

when charged then answered 'no'. Mr E. Clayton for the Director of Public Prosecutions, said Mrs Brewer and her daughter were found dead with head wounds apparently inflicted with a hammer, at Mrs Brewer's flat at Grove Flats, Ealing.

On the arm of the dead woman's chair was found a note. It stated 'Dear Ernie, I am sorry to do this to you and please God forgive me, but I am afraid your wife is very immoral. We are going the same way soon, and I hope just as quickly. We don't know you personally but we know your heart and believe me when you get over the shock you will be better off. God forgive us.' The letter was unsigned.

After statements alleged to have been made by both the accused had been read, the magistrates retired. Later, the chairman, Mr Cully, announced that the case against Mrs Koopman was dismissed. She was assisted from the court.

In his statement Koopman was alleged to have said, 'I love my wife and baby very much and what I have done was when I was not in my right state of mind.'

Mr Clayton added that at Ealing police station Koopman said, 'It had nothing to do with my wife. I did it and I am prepared to pay for it. Shirley was crying, and I thought it was no good leaving her without her mother.'

Koopman continued in his alleged statement to say that he first met Gladys Brewer about five years ago and found that she was of a loose type. He met Gladys Brewer again 12 months ago and introduced her to his wife. On 5 September he was given week-end leave and was to be posted to Bridlington.

His wife hated the idea of his going away, and they decided to run away together. They decided to go to Viney's (Mrs Brewer's) house.

On 8 September Mrs Koopman and he went out drinking and came back feeling the effect of it. Mr Clayton said that the statement went on, 'I began to tease Viney by putting the gas down while she was trying to read. She cried, "Stop it." I suppose that at that moment I thought of all the bad things against her.

'I took a hammer with the intent to frighten her. I know I struck her on the head with a hammer. My wife said, "Don't do it." She grabbed my arm to stop me. Then I heard the baby Shirley crying.

'I took the torch into the bedroom and struck the child with the hammer repeatedly until she stopped crying. We thought the best thing to do was to clear away.'

The alleged statement went on: 'We took a few shillings and coppers from Viney's purse. I took the rings off Viney's fingers. I wrote a note to Viney's husband.

'What I have done I would not have done in my right state of mind. It must have been the drink I had.'

A newspaper report of 5 October 1943 under the headline DOUBLE MURDER: AIRCRAFTMAN SENT FOR TRIAL went as follows:

Divisional Detective-inspector W. Tarr said he found the body of Mrs Brewer in an armchair. There was bloodstained RAF clothing in the room, and an RAF tunic was behind her head.

At Slough police station Koopman inquired about Mrs Brewer's husband and said, 'I expect he will come with a sten gun, and I don't blame him.'

When asked what had happened to the child's pram, Koopman said, 'We wanted some money. There was only a shilling and a few coppers in her (Mrs Brewer's) handbag. My wife took the rings off her fingers, and as the baby was asleep in the pram we took that too. The wife sold the rings and the pram in shops at West Drayton.'

A newspaper report of 15 December 1943 said under the headline EXECUTED FOR DOUBLE MURDER Charles William Koopman aged 23, aircraftman of Hanwell was executed at Pentonville Prison today for the murder of Mrs Gladys Levina Brewer, aged 22 and her two-year-old daughter Shirley, at Ealing.

'Koopman killed Mrs Brewer and her daughter with a hammer. At the Old Bailey the defence was a plea of insanity.

Above
The 'Haunted Hall':
Christ Church Parish
Hall, known as Buckell
Hall

Right
The house where Mrs
Gladys Brewer was
murdered

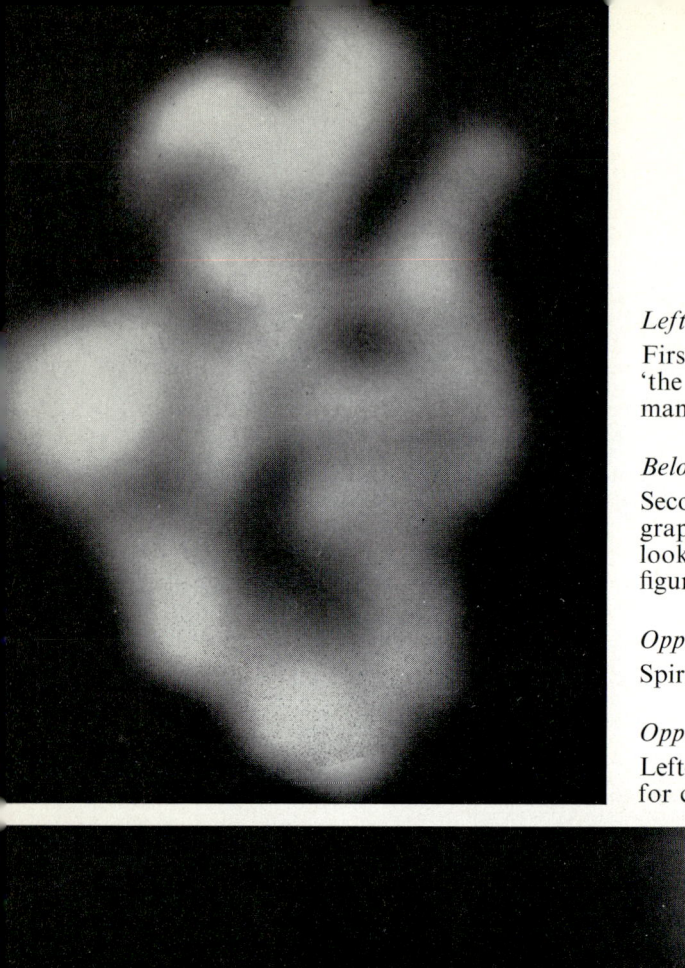

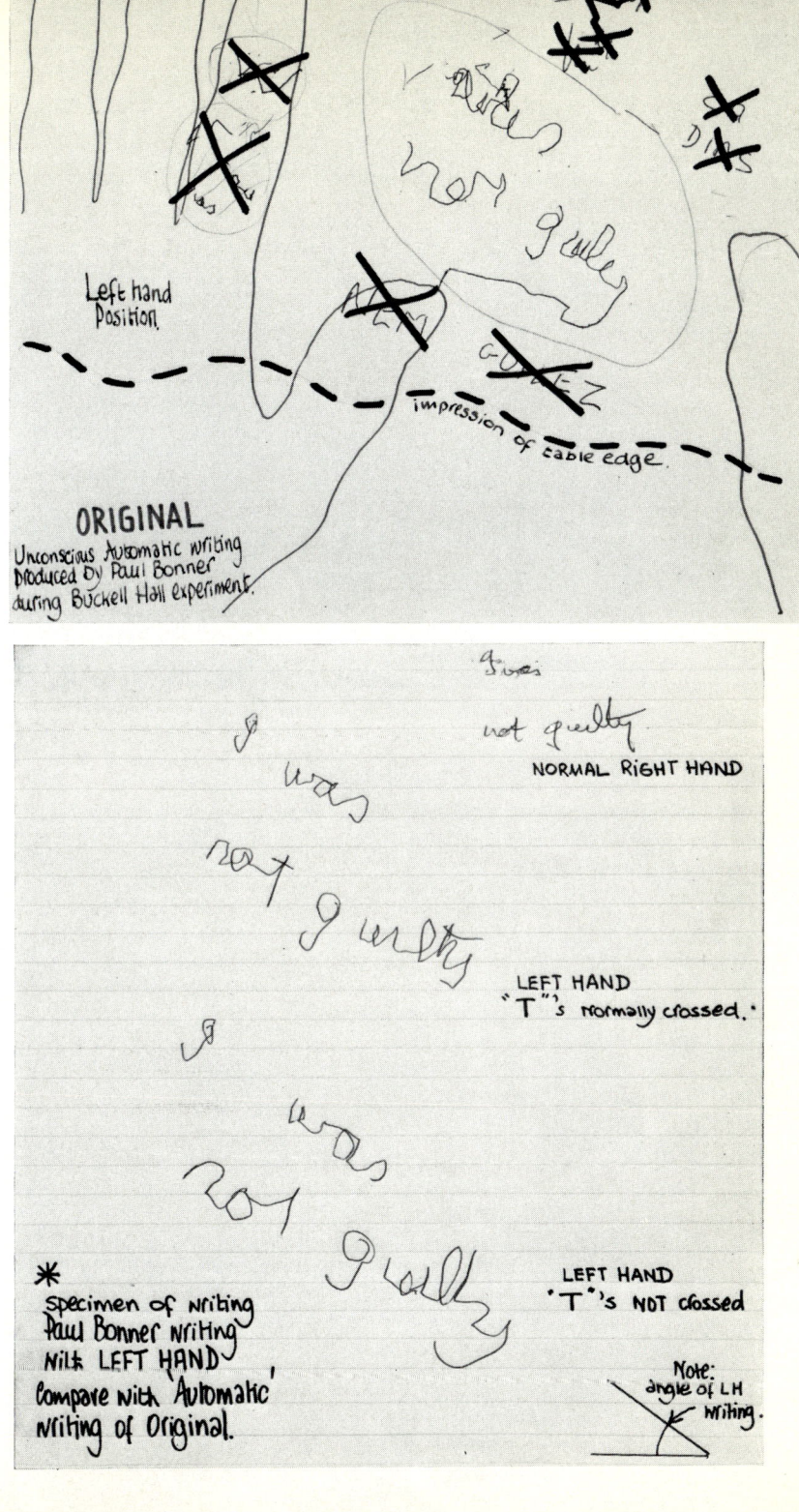

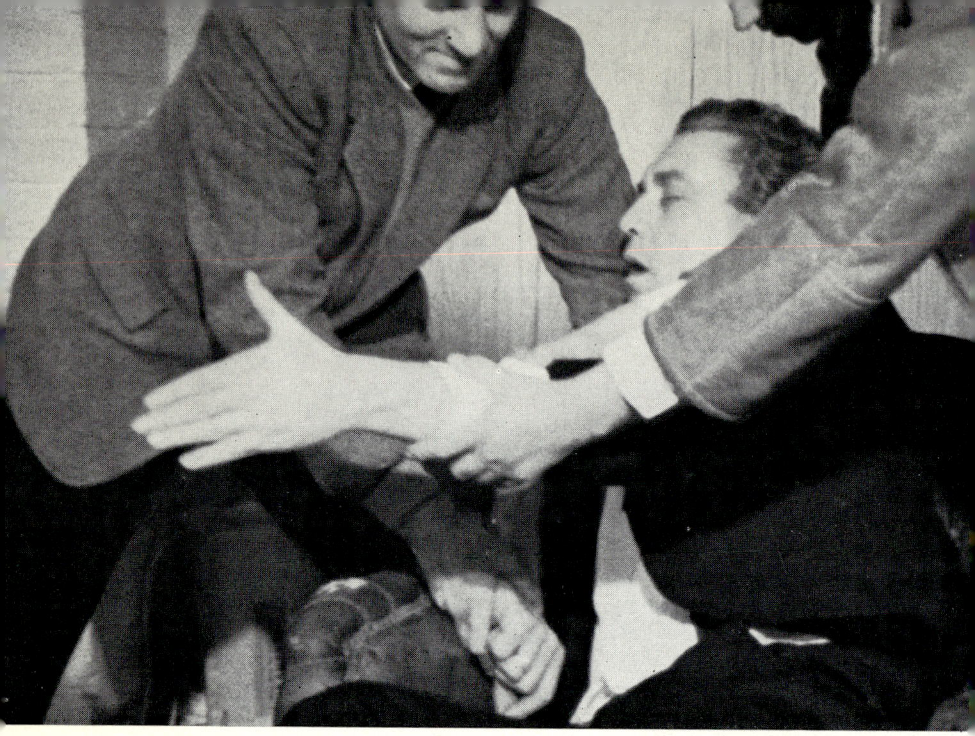

Above George in a trance

Below 'Six great scratches criss-crossed over the skin'

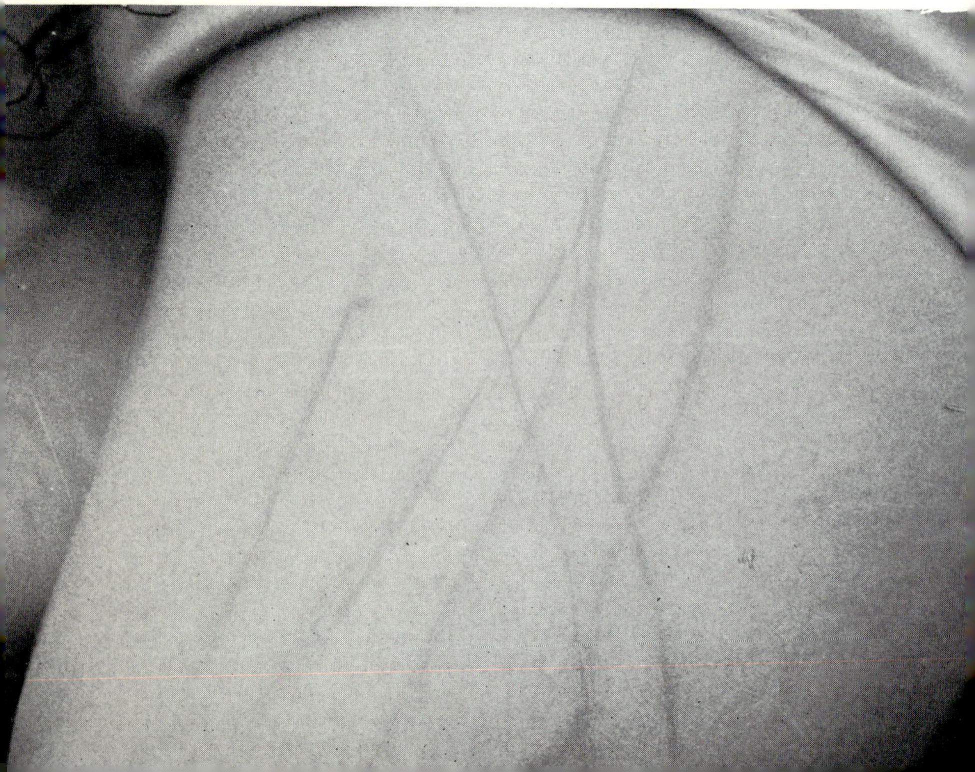

Evidence was given that Koopman was suffering from a rare disease of the mind.'

I have given these reports at length because of the bearing which this tragic case seemed to have on much of what followed at Buckell Hall, the place (according to the police) where Shirley's battered pram – presumably after recovery from a West Drayton junk shop – had been stored. The pram seems to me to have an important bearing on the case: it was the actual scene of the murder of the child. Koopman in his statement said he had killed the child in the bedroom and that 'the baby was asleep in the pram.' The inference is that Shirley was murdered in the pram and the pram, the scene of the crime, was later moved into Buckell Hall.

I now take up again the interrupted story of the seance held by the SPR members in Buckell Hall on 23 July 1965. The substance of rapped messages was that Margaret, two years of age, had been murdered by her father in 1937 in Buckell Hall. She is now with her mother (who by inference has also to be dead) and is a Catholic.

At one point during the sitting 'Margaret' was asked to demonstrate that she was in fact there by giving a sign for all present to perceive. After a short pause there was a loud crash in the corner of the room near Bob Saunders. Subsequently he found that one of his two microphones had left its position on the enlarger table and had hit the floor behind him some five or six feet away from its previous position.

Bob Saunders has from his RAF service days been a professional radiophonics engineer. After the seance, he examined his two recordings with a good deal of curiosity and interest. He found that *recording A* had a repetitive stroking noise at a very high level near the start of the sitting. A whispering voice very close to the microphone (he estimated the source to be only 1 inch away) appears and later on, when George Medhurst is heard inviting 'Margaret' to 'show some sign', the stroking appears immediately as if 'on cue', again at a very high volume but rather more continuous in character. The noise stops and the sound of *microphone B* hitting the floor is clearly on *A*.

On *recording B* there is no trace at all of the stroking noise. The whispering voice appears at the same moment in time as on *A* and is identical but the voice is accompanied by a rhythmical, distinct tapping noise: further on in the recording the tapping appears again and sounds to some people like wings flapping. This sound does not appear on *recording A*. When the *B* microphone hits the floor it stops recording momentarily.

A table will show the situation at a glance:

Recording A	*Recording B*
Repetitive stroking noise at very high level at beginning	No stroking noise
Whispering voice very close on microphone	Whispering voice appears but is accompanied by tapping noise
Stroking noise appears on cue when George Medhurst asks for 'a sign'	
Stroking noise stops and sounds of microphone B hitting the floor can be heard	Recording stops momentarily as microphone B hits the floor

Saunders afterwards made a number of tests on the microphones. He found he could reproduce deliberately the stroking effect and whispering voice on microphone *A*, but it was difficult to gauge the required intensity of sound which would record but not be heard by others present in a small room (such as the darkroom). On microphone *B*, the tapping or flapping sound can also be deliberately produced by handling the microphone in a certain way, but it is not easy to do without moving it and creating further and more obvious noise. He found it extremely difficult to judge the exact volume necessary to whisper and tap at the same time without making enough noise to record on the other microphone, or even be heard in a small room.

In a report written on 9 August 1965 (i.e. less than a month after the seance) from which the above events have been abstracted, Saunders goes on to say:

If the sounds were originated by someone in the room it

would have been very difficult to locate the microphones accurately in the dark (no groping or fumbling noises are present). I would also have thought that the risk of perpetrating such an obvious hoax would have been great. The room was for most of the time completely silent, however I must confess that I suspected George, (i.e. the photographer – *not* George Medhurst) of having consciously or unconsciously produced the noises, by very skilful means for reasons best known only to himself. I would have thought that some specialised knowledge of microphones and recording equipment would have been necessary to produce the effects I have mentioned – George does not have this.

I practised for some considerable time before I could achieve just the right intensity of sound necessary to *record* but not to be heard acoustically – but I would not even attempt such an experiment in a completely dark room.

On Thursday 29 July a sitting was held at Buckell Hall to which no members of the SPR were invited although Miss Barrington was told it would take place. Those present were George, Rita, Ann (Rita's cousin), Anne Whillock (my BBC secretary) and Bob Saunders. The session was played out with a table in total darkness. Rita suggested beforehand that Anne Whillock and Saunders should sit either side of George, their principal suspect. After a long period of no response, everyone said they could feel distinct gusts of cold air on their hands. Several times these gusts occurred while George was actually speaking and Saunders reports 'by a process of elimination I proved that no one member of the group was blowing by mouth. Occasional quite strong cold draughts were felt on our faces. The room had previously been sealed by stopping door cracks; the only window in the room is permanently "light" sealed for photographic reasons.'

At last, definite but weak 'contact' was established with 'Margaret', the table answering 'yes' and 'no' to random questions. When asked if 'she' required to speak to someone in the room, the table rapped out RED HAIR. Anne Whillock was the one person present with red hair but nothing apparently significant to those present resulted from the ensuing conversation. At one point, the table rose up from the floor several inches. Immediately this happened, George clasped Saunders' and Anne Whillock's hands and lifted them up away from the table as if to say 'It's not me' – or, 'Is it you ?' although nothing was actually said at the time.

The table remained suspended and Saunders was able to push it down but it rose again and remained aloft for several seconds. They were able to discuss the phenomena and experience the rather spongy 'feel' at will. Saunders wrote '(George) was not responsible for this apparent levitation and I am at a loss to explain it'.

On Wednesday 4 August another sitting was held with exactly the same people as the week before: George, Rita, Ann, Anne Whillock and Saunders. At Rita's suggestion, the table was set up in the body of the hall. A circle of cards with letters from A to Z was placed round the perimeter of the table and the group placed fingers on an upturned drinking glass in the manner of the well-known Ouija board type party game. But nothing happened. They then tried the hands on table routine with all lights on. Getting no response, they tried again with the lights switched off. Once more no response. At Rita's suggestion they lifted their hands from the table and linked them forming a circle with just enough light filtering into the hall from the street lamps to allow them to keep an eye on things. Shortly Rita showed marked signs of distress and Ann, her cousin, 'thought' she could see an outline of a figure at the back of the hall, but could have been mistaken. Rita became even more distressed and the circle was broken and the lights put on.

When things had calmed down, the group retired to the small darkroom and made another attempt at communication through the table, in darkness. At first there was no result and then Ann suggested 'forming a circle' again though Rita was reluctant but agreed when pressed. After a short time, Rita again exhibited considerable distress and when the light was switched on she was trembling and upset. She suddenly cried out and said that a grey mist was obscuring her vision and, says

Saunders, 'she looked really very frightened indeed'. Anne Whillock succeeded in calming Rita down and Saunders suggested packing up. George, however, insisted that they carry on and that Rita was all right. With some reluctance, they made another attempt to achieve contact by means of the table in total darkness. The table was asked if there was a message for anyone present. The table spelt G.S. Rita asked if this was intended to be George. The reply was YES. The table then rocked out the following message: SOON BE WITH ME. Rita asked who was speaking ? The reply was DEAD. Question: Is it Margaret ? No response. Have you a message ? The reply was G.S. (pause) SOON BE DEAD. Saunders reported 'We then abandoned the sitting, feeling that perhaps a rather sinister element had pervaded the meeting.'

During these sittings Bob Saunders had been proceeding on lines indicated by Dr Dingwall and as agreed by me in order to collect material for a programme which I had virtually sold to my long-standing colleague and friend David Attenborough who at that time was Controller of BBC 2. However, because Saunders was still on the BBC strength as a dubbing mixer and was acting in the capacity of a programme assistant on attachment, our immediate BBC superior was unwilling to allow Saunders a completely free hand and insisted on bringing in a trusted and tried BBC television producer. This was Paul Bonner.

So Saunders arranged the next sitting at the hall (on 26 August 1965) to include Paul Bonner and his secretary Sarah Glover. The group was completed by the usual sitters, George, Rita, Ann, Anne Whillock and Saunders. This proved to be a significant meeting.

The group formed a circle in the darkroom in complete darkness. After fifteen minutes of no response, Saunders experienced a persistent and recurrent thought; the name HENRY MEADOWS, which meant nothing to him but persuaded him to ask 'Does the name Henry Meadows mean anything to anyone ?' The reply was no. Then Paul Bonner said, 'A ridiculous feeling for a sceptical man, but I suddenly feel that

there's nothing here anymore – just us sitting alone.' They
placed their hands on the table and immediately felt cold
draughts over them. When requested the table moved from side
to side over the floor, sometimes very violently, sometimes
twisting. It was a small table, but a 'period' one and heavy. It
did not at this stage lift or levitate. When Rita asked, 'Is there
anyone here tonight?' distinct knocks or taps were heard, not
from the table, but from the direction of the green door. Rita
continued, 'Is it a man here tonight?' Table: YES. 'Is your
name Henry Meadows?' No reply. Then the table rapped B
(or YES) DETH. Rita asked 'Are you trying to spell "death"?'
Table: YES. Next George complained of 'something' rubbing
his hair. Paul Bonner the television producer smelled tobacco
'like an old pipe'. George complained of a 'terrible hot sensation' on the side of his face and exclaimed 'Good Lord! My
face!' Ann then asked for the lights to be put on being worried
by a smell. The lights were switched on when the following
dialogue occurred:

Ann: The smell – you will laugh at me if I tell you what
I think it was: brimstone!
Bonner: Come, come! How would you know what brim-
stone is, or what it smelled like?
Ann: It was like sulphur. A musty smell.
Bonner: It was like the inside of the bowl of a very old pipe
to me.

Saunders had noticed when the lights were switched on that
'three "angry" scratches had appeared on the right side of
(George's) face. Surprisingly they were not noticed or referred
to by anyone. I thought this odd, but I didn't say anything
either.'

After some time they put out the light once more and
resumed the sitting. The table then began to move, on request,
in almost any direction. When asked, it moved to Ann, to Rita,
to George quite firmly; it rose from the floor and at one point
pinned Anne Whillock and Bob Saunders against the enlarger,
finally moving back and lifting up. By this stage Paul Bonner
and Bob Saunders were pressing down in an attempt to restrain

the table but their efforts had no effect. The table apparently hesitated, moved from side to side and twisted in the air. It then began to rock violently and by the usual means of rocking by numbers the following dialogue took place:

1. *Table*: VFP ... VOILEMNT
2. *Group*: discussed whether 'viola', 'violet' etc was intended and then asked 'Is it violent ?'
3. *Table*: YES. SO THE THTOUR
4. *Group*: Is it 'Violent so they thought'?
5. *Table*: YES. I WO
6. *Group*: Is it 'would' ?
7. *Table*: YES. MILL.
8. *Group*: Is it K instead of M ?
9. *Table*: YES. M.
10. *Group*: Is it Margaret ?
11. *Table*: YES.

The group discussed the final wording and came to the conclusion, at the time, that the message they had received was: VIOLENT SO THOUGHT I WOULD KILL MARGARET. They had, in fact, forgotten the word 'they' noted in 3, 4 and 5 above, an omission which produces a message quite different from the true meaning and which assumes a great significance in view of what subsequently happened at this session. Saunders' attention was only drawn to the missing THE (Y) when he listened afterwards to the tape-recording.

The dialogue with the table continued:

1. *Rita*: Who is speaking to us ?
2. *Table*: G E
3. *Rita*: Is it George ?
4. *Table*: YES.
5. *Saunders*: George *Meadows* ?
6. *Table*: YES.
7. *Rita*: Are you with us all the time ?
8. *Table*: YES.
9. *Rita*: Do you live in this room particularly ?
10. *Table*: YES.
11. *Rita*: Do you like us to speak to you ?

12.	*Table:*	YES.
13.	*Rita:*	Whereabouts do you usually stand in this room – is it by the green door ?
14.	*Table:*	YES.
15.	*Rita:*	And do you also stand by the sink ?
16.	*Table:*	YES.
17.	*Rita:*	Do you give us this cold feeling when you're in here ?
18.	*Table:*	(No response)
19.	*Rita:*	Are you always here ?
20.	*Table:*	NO . . .
21.	*Rita:*	How many years ago did you kill Margaret ?
22.	*Table:*	THIRTY (1935)
23.	*Rita:*	Is Margaret here with you ?
24.	*Table:*	YES.
25.	*Rita:*	Margaret is here with you all the time ?

(No sooner had this question been asked than the sitters felt a cold wind)

26.	*Rita:*	Is the wind Margaret ?
27.	*Table:*	YES.

(Cold wind felt by all present)

28.	*Rita:*	Hallo Margaret! You are with us too ?
29.	*Table:*	YES.
30.	*Rita:*	Is it Margaret that does the naughty things ?
31.	*Table:*	YES.
32.	*Rita:*	Is Margaret's mother here with you ?
33.	*Table:*	YES.
34.	*Rita:*	Will you spell us her name ?
35.	*Table:*	s (Q)

(Cold wind)

36.	*Saunders:*	Is it Susan ?
37.	*Table:*	YES.
38.	*Rita:*	Is Susan here with you, George ?
39.	*Table:*	YES.
40.	*Ann:*	Are you a Roman Catholic ?
41.	*Table:*	YES.
42.	*Rita:*	George, are you smoking a pipe ?

43.	*Table*:	YES.
(Cold wind)		
44.	*Rita*:	Were you an airman ?
45.	*Table*:	YES.
46.	*Rita*:	Were you married to Susan ?
47.	*Table*:	YES.
48.	*Rita*:	Then her name is Susan Meadows ?
49.	*Table*:	YES.
50.	*Rita*:	Was Margaret two years old when she died ?
51.	*Table*:	YES.
52.	*George*:	George, did you have a girl friend apart from Susan ?
53.	*Table*:	NO.
54.	*Rita*:	Which month of the year did you kill Margaret ?
55.	*Table*:	(No response)
56.	*Rita*:	Did you kill Margaret in December ?
57.	*Table*:	(No response)
58.	*Rita*:	Did you murder Margaret in December?
59.	*Table*:	(No response)
60.	*Rita*:	When you killed Margaret was it January of the year ?
61.	*Table*:	(No response)
62.	*Rita*:	February ?
63.	*Table*:	(No response)

(In view of what happened later at this sitting, the lack of response to questions 54, 56, 58, 60 and 62 assumes some significance).

64.	*Rita*:	Are you happy having George and I working here ?
65.	*Table*:	NO.
66.	*Rita*:	Do you like the music we play here ?
67.	*Table*:	YES.
68.	*Rita*:	Do you like the flowers we put out for you ?
69.	*Table*:	YES (or possibly 3 raps)
70.	*Rita*:	As a group, as we're sitting round the table

		now, would you like us to come here again ?
71.	*Table*:	YES.
72.	*Rita*:	Would you like us to come again soon ?
73.	*Table*:	YES.
74.	*Rita*:	Is Margaret still here with us ?

(Cold wind, very strong)

75.	*Rita*:	Is Susan with us here too ?
76.	*Table*:	YES.
77.	*Rita*:	Can she do something now, please ?
78.	*Table*:	YES.
79.	*Rita*:	Now then please, Susan.

(The table then rocked from the other side to which it had been turning so far. At this point the tape recorder battery failed).

After the lights had been put on, Bob Saunders suggested a trial of automatic writing as an experiment. This method of obtaining information is well-known, there being many mediums who specialise in writing automatically messages from the 'other side' during periods of light trance. Whether a random group of sitters could hope to produce automatic writing is doubtful. Saunders distributed pencils and blank sheets of paper to all the sitters except Paul Bonner and Ann who preferred to use their own ball-point pens. It was agreed that the pens or pencils should be held upright with the point touching the paper. The free hand was used to steady the paper on the table. The lights were switched off ; nothing appeared to happen.

The silence lasted for several minutes and was suddenly broken by a loud clatter. Paul Bonner exclaimed, 'My biro has been knocked out of my hand! I'm afraid there isn't much chance of finding it. It's probably on the floor.'

Several more minutes elapsed and Saunders, feeling his experiment was a failure, called for the lights to be switched on.

When the lights came up, Paul Bonner was heard to exclaim 'But this is incredible!'

Saunders saw that both Bonner's hands were flat down on

his piece of paper and between his hands was written by ball-point pen a message which was interpreted to be I WAS NOT GUILTY. This paper, which is now in my possession, is repro-duced in photos five and six. Paul Bonner's biro was found in the middle of the table.

As can be seen from the figure, in addition to the spidery writing in the middle there are attempts at first interpretations which Saunders later crossed out. At first the top line seemed to Bonner to represent CA DIAS and the bottom line NEM GUILEZ, which he wrote on the paper. That is to say, if he *did* write the spidery squiggle then he must have done it unconsciously because the conscious part of his mind failed at first to offer a sensible transliteration.

But did Bonner write the 'message'? Only last Monday, 15 January 1973, I asked Paul Bonner to account for what hap-pened. He did not know how the message had appeared on the paper but accepted that he had in fact written it without consciously knowing. In a report written four days after the sitting Saunders said:

If the message was written right way up it could have been over Paul Bonner's left shoulder. It was not unconscious automatic writing because the pen was missing. (*This con-clusion does not follow, because the message could have been written before the pen clattered out of Bonner's hand*). No other member of the group 'produced' a message – although everyone scribbled a little, except George who was out of the group (for reasons I do not consider significant[1]) and did not take part. For the record, he was sitting away from the table in the opposite corner to Bonner and could not have interfered with the experiment.

Having explained automatic writing to the group – it was practically an invitation to the 'impressionable' or 'conscious' to write almost anything under the guise of automatic writ-ing. If the writing was in fact unconscious manipulation how

[1]Sarah Glover, Bonner's secretary had offended George by plain speaking and he felt he was being suspected of fakery and so retired from the circle.

did the message appear in three inches of space between Paul Bonner's hands without fumbling or making any sound in the dark ?

I take it from this that at the time Saunders was of the opinion that Bonner had not written the message, nor had any other living person in the room, but that some other perpetrator was responsible. I see no logical reason why, if poltergeist energy can move furniture, a table, an oilcan it cannot move a ball-point pen and make it write. But I do not believe that this happened here. I believe, with Bonner, that he produced the writing unconsciously, and Saunders himself in a careful, indeed scientific way, made this conclusion the inevitable one. Saunders drew round Bonner's fingers to indicate their position on the paper. He also marked with a dotted line the pie-crust edge of the 'period' table. In addition, when the group had come to the conclusion that the message was I WAS NOT GUILTY, Saunders got Bonner to write this sentence three times (photo 6): once in his normal right hand, once with his left hand with the 't's' crossed, and once with his left hand with the 't's' uncrossed. The third specimen is to all intents and purposes identical with the 'automatic' message.

Saunders concluded his report of 30 August with the words: 'The message "I was not guilty" did not really make sense until we restored the missing "THEY" to the first message *afterwards*. The result: VIOLENT SO THEY THOUGHT I WOULD KILL MARGARET – I WAS NOT GUILTY.'

On 31 August Bob Saunders wrote to George Medhurst of the SPR and in the course of his letter said:

Our last meeting at Buckell Hall was on Thursday of last week, 26 August. I introduced two further members to the group, Paul Bonner (a BBC producer) and Sarah Glover (secretary to Paul). Paul Bonner has taken over production responsibility for any programme which may ensue from these investigations. I remain on as Research Assistant and film director, but it seems likely that the programme we originally envisaged is 'not on' – I am convinced that we are on to something, but what ? I intend to continue with these researches whether we go on with the programme or not because I am personally intrigued by the whole business.

On Thursday 2 September Paul Bonner attended a second sitting at Buckell Hall. Also present were George, Rita, Anne Whillock and Bob Saunders. The only phenomena worth noting were some weak cold draughts.

Five days later, 7 September, Bonner wrote to the Head of BBC Television Features recommending that the idea of a television programme be dropped. He gave two reasons: (1) the incidents at Buckell Hall would not provide the sort of programme that Controller BBC2 required for Halloween, and (2) such a programme as could be made would have extremely unfortunate consequences on (George's) private life and business. In his letter he said nothing about his own strange experience.

Bob Saunders was not, of course, going to give up, as his letter to George Medhurst showed. In any case, he knew that I was due back from my sabbatical leave within a couple of weeks and would not only expect an accounting from him but would be only too eager to push forward the investigations. So Saunders called another meeting at Buckell Hall for 8.15 pm 10 September 1965. The sitters were George, Rita, Ann, Anne Whillock and Bob Saunders. The observation equipment was one tape recorder with a cardioid microphone padded with sponge rubber and attached to the table top ; and a quarter-plate camera. The procedure with the camera was to leave the shutter open with the lens at full aperture during the periods when the lights were out.

The significance of this particular seance, in my opinion, resides in three things: (1) the difficulty which the communicant or communicants had in 'getting through' (2) the violence exhibited by the table and (3) the behaviour of Rita.

The difficulty of communication expressed itself in a number of ways: there were raps which the sitters did not hear but which were recorded on tape ; there was constant fumbling in the spelling out of words ; at least twice the table rapped through the whole alphabet, i.e. twenty-six times. It is tempting to put an anthropomorphic interpretation on the table's violence. A human being might well have felt deeply frustrated at not getting through, in being thwarted and so expressed his frustration in violence. At any rate, Bob Saunders reported:

> Very violent and alarming table movement occurred and finished up by the table falling over on its side towards Rita and Anne Whillock. It then moved very violently sideways on the floor knocking George over and stopped underneath the enlarger .... Table moved violently sideways. *Rita*: 'Would you spell to us please? ' Table moved to Rita. *Rita*: 'Please lift the table right off the floor.' Table rocked very violently. Alarm expressed by all sitters. Table turned over on its side violently. *George*: 'This is getting out of hand!' *Rita*: 'Will you try and lift the table right off the floor.' Table lifted right UP and then DOWN .... Table shot violently with considerable velocity across the floor to George knocking him sideways off his chair.

Not unnaturally, they put the light on. All during this sitting everyone noticed frequent cold draughts. After the early table violence the microphone had been removed to the enlarger table ; before the break periods, when the lights were switched on, the camera had been closed. No exposures were recorded.

It was then about 10.45 pm. The table appeared to address Rita with a message which they interpreted as RITA TO SPEAK. After a time the group joined hands above the table and Rita complained of feeling 'funny' as if she was 'going off'. Then they got a message which the table confirmed as I STAND NEAR YOU. They asked if the communicant was George Meadows and the table rapped YES. Then the word FEAR came, followed by MUST I KILL YOU. Rita reacted to this by saying 'No you must not! It's not necessary for me to k ... – for you to kill me, but if you want, I don't! I'm not frightened of you but I don't want to see you by dying. I'd like to see you by sitting here. Speaking to you – can you show yourself to me?' The table rapped YES. 'Will you show yourself to me tonight ?' YES. 'Would you like to show yourself to me now, George ?' YES. 'Would you like us to form a circle?' (i.e. link hands above the table) YES. George the photographer then said, 'Well, I don't fancy it, personally.' Ann said, 'Is he going to use someone as a medium or by himself?' Rita: 'Will you appear by yourself?' NO. Rita: 'You want to use me as the medium?' YES. George the photographer: 'Well, we're not doing that! That's for sure!' Rita: 'George, would you show yourself through another medium?' NO. George the photographer: 'Well that's it! That's as far as we go!' Rita: 'I'm sorry George. I couldn't go into a trance. I couldn't help you. I don't think I could. Could we adjourn for a little while?'

The lights were switched on and discussion followed, Rita being willing to offer herself as a medium and George the photographer being against such a trial. However, the group did put the lights out and Rita said 'Will you appear through me if you want to?' There were some violent raps, some cold draughts, but soon the report concluded with the words: 'General feeling that "George" had abandoned us.'

I think that after this sitting there was an expectation that something dramatic was likely to happen before very long. Bob Saunders felt that the drama would centre on Rita. In a letter dated 14 September (i.e. four days after the sitting) to Miss Mary Rose Barrington of the SPR, Saunders wrote 'I must tell you about the risk (if any) of trance, as I believe (Rita) is possibly a "natural" medium and could achieve such a state but is worried by the consequences.' In fact the drama, when it did come, was explosive, shocking and did not concern Rita except as a bystander. I myself was present and can give an eyewitness account supported by a tape-recording. Before that, however, I feel this is the point to discuss a little more fully the method of extracting communications via the table.

Most reasonable people who know of table-rapping from hearsay and what they have read, people who have never practised it, believe the procedure to be fraught with fakery and ridiculous. Reasonable people with experience of table-rapping and with open minds about Psi-phenomena appear to explain the rocking of the table by holding the sitters responsible: if faking is employed, then one or more of the sitters is pushing or lifting the table with intent ; if faking is absent, then one or more of the sitters is pushing or lifting the table unconsciously. Another theory (where fraud is discounted) suggests that the table is moved by rods or cantilevers of aetherial substance, ectoplasm, call it what you will, proceeding from the body of a medium present among the sitters ; movement by 'Odic' force is yet another explanation.[1]

In a case like ours, I feel one can only argue from personal experience. I myself was later to join the Buckell Hall group and take part in table-rocking over a period of three months. At first the sessions were in darkness, later we found the table would rock with lights on and in front of a movie-camera. From my experience, I start at the beginning by asserting that the table actually *moved* – sometimes not only rocking but shooting violently as far as it could go in the confined space of the darkroom, say four or five feet across the floor. I witnessed a violence in the table sufficient to knock Bob Saunders and his chair over backwards on to the ground: Shall I ever forget the look of hurt, frightened astonishment on his face ? Nobody likes to be attacked, but to be attacked by an inanimate object is disturbing. My next assertion is that although I was constantly on the look-out for fraud, I never saw anyone moving or lifting the table consciously ; nor do I believe any member of the group was unconsciously manipulating it ; finally, I do not believe in, and certainly never saw, a rod or cantilever of ectoplasm which might move the table. It would have been possible to focus a time-lapse movie-camera on the table in the darkroom, move everyone out, start the camera rolling, seal the doors and windows from the outside and leave for a period or hours. I don't think such an experiment would have got us very far, for I don't believe the table would have moved. Nevertheless, the experiment *is* perhaps worth doing, for if the table moves it is possible to assert that a table can rock without sitters either (a) pushing it consciously or (b) pushing it unconsciously or (c) moving it by any other means. If the table does *not* move, then the most one can say is that it appears necessary to have sitters before movement will take place.

[1] See page 68 above

My own belief (for what it is worth) is that a table with a group of sitters will *not* move unless one or more is capable of poltergeist mediumstry: and I assert that these capabilities are commoner than we might think. I do not believe that the movement in non-fraudulent cases is caused by conscious or unconscious pushing. I do believe that the movement proceeds from a power which the poltergeist medium is capable of producing or 'plugging in to' unconsciously. It follows therefore, in my theory that the movement comes from the mind of the waking medium, and from that part of the mind which functions below the level of consciousness. What motivates or triggers off the medium's unconscious mind to make a table rap out messages is anybody's guess ; but if my theory is correct, then the next question we need to answer is, is the motivation interior or exterior ? In other words, is it automatic or does something outside the medium cause it ?

I don't think there is much to be gained by theorising further at the moment: when I come to the last chapter of this book I hope to be able to add to what I have just said.

Just after the last sitting at Buckell Hall reported above, my family and I arrived back in England from our long holiday in Europe. I was not dismayed when Bob Saunders told me that Paul Bonner had opted out and that he had begun to run the sittings without professional mediums or the SPR being present. I arranged to be present at the next meeting together with my wife Dodo and a date was fixed for 1 October 1965.

Both Dodo and I were pleasantly apprehensive when we joined the others that Friday evening in Buckell Hall. Anne Whillock my secretary had gone home for the weekend and of the other regular sitters I had not met Rita's cousin Ann before ; Dodo had not met any of them.

We sat down at about 8.30 pm in the small darkroom at the back of the hall. Those present were George, Rita, Ann, Bob Saunders, Dodo and myself. My first impression was of the cramped space. The enlarger on its bench faced me and took up at least a square yard of floor space. My back was to a huge washing tank about 5ft by 2½ft and 4ft high. There was a door in the right-hand wall leading to a print drying room, lavatory and tiny kitchen, and a door (the famous green door) in the left-hand wall leading to a narrow passage connecting the main studio to the outside back door. Across this narrow passage was another tiny processing room. The dark room red 'safe light' was on the wall to my right; the main room light hung from the middle of the ceiling and there dangled down a bathroom type cord to switch the light off and on.

The 'antique' type table with a circular pie-crust top had been changed for a small rectangular table with four legs which was set between the enlarger bench and the washing tank and midway between the two doors. Because the group invariably sat in the same places during the following meetings (up to the fateful final one) I attach a diagram showing where each person normally sat on assorted light 'kitchen' chairs:

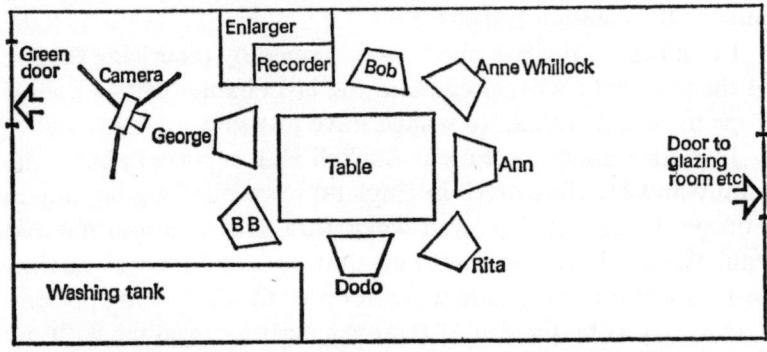

Sometimes the three girls, Ann, Rita and Anne Whillock would change places, but Dodo always sat next to me, I always sat on George's right and Bob Saunders always sat on George's left. Because George was the principal suspect, Saunders and I made it our business to watch him or, when the lights were out, to maintain contact with him. I always sat with my left leg in contact with George's right one, and with my left hand in contact with his right. Saunders similarly kept contact with George's left hand and leg. Of course, he knew we suspected him and while none of us overtly voiced suspicions, except on one or two very special occasions, George would frequently raise both Saunders' and my hands off the table during rocking to show that he, at least, wasn't manipulating the table.

On this particular Friday night it had been arranged to set up the still camera again because Rita believed that 'George' was going to materialise. The camera, a quarter plate MPP 5x4, Schneider Xenar W/a lens was set up on a very substantial metal tripod immediately behind George and in between him and the green door. There was a panning head with a handle about two feet long and the camera having been pointed over George the photographer's head towards the table, the panning head was locked. George was using Kodak plus-X cut film and because it seemed too chancy for flash equipment the camera had to be ready to catch anything at any time – *by itself* – so the procedure was as follows. The lens was set at full aperture, F.6.3 ; the lens cap was left on ; the shutter was opened. As soon as the sitters were in their places and the lights turned out, George was allowed to raise his left-hand from the table and remove the lens cap, placing it on the enlarger bench – the work at most of two seconds. The camera would then be exposing in complete darkness and unless a light-reflecting object appeared, nothing should be recorded on the film ; for George would replace the lens cap just before we were ready to switch the lights on again.

In addition to the camera, the proceedings were, as usual, taped on a Philips recorder using a cardioid microphone.

We began a sitting in complete darkness and the usual sitters mentioned feeling cold draughts. Dodo felt them too. The table began to rock and spelled out a message from 'George' with the news that he intended 'to appear on the film.' Naturally we were all very interested by this information and after some thirty minutes our George was asked to break the contact with the table and replace the lens cap on the camera. He did this and the light was pulled on. George took the film from the camera and went alone through the green door, across the entry to the processing room ; shortly returned with the dripping film processed and fixed, and as he stepped inside, his eyes were bulging and he said gaspingly 'There's something on it! There's something on it!' He plunged the negative into the washing tank and we all crowded to the edge. A milky, bulbous border nearly filled the quarter plate with a dark negative image in the middle. I looked at George and said, 'You bugger! You faked it!'

He denied it strenuously, his eyes still popping, and we all argued furiously. When you turned the negative in a certain direction it appeared to be the head of an old man with deep set eyes, a long lock of hair and an open mouth.

Before I comment on this photograph, I want to relate what happened subsequently. Of course, we all wanted to 'test' what had taken place and (like budding scientists) repeat the experiment. We watched George take a film out of what we believed was the packet which he had freshly opened to extract the first film. He put it into the camera under the stern gaze of us all. We took our places at the table going through exactly the same procedure as before. When the lights were out George removed the lens cap and before long the table was rapping out a series of communications from 'George', 'Margaret' and 'Susan'.

After half an hour or so we decided to break. The lens cap was replaced by George and the lights were switched on. Before the film was taken from the camera I stood behind George and gripped his wrists individually with my left hand on his left wrist and my right hand on his right wrist. I continued with this hold during the whole processing of this particular negative. We walked together through the green door in step like a couple of old-time music hall comics. We crossed the passage into the processing room and somebody shut the door behind us. I never let go my grip all the time that he was processing and fixing the film in the dark in that little room, moving his hands from one pan with photographic chemicals to another all by sense of feel, for we did not even have a 'safe' light on. When he was done we marched out again and joined the others eagerly waiting. Nor was their expectancy dashed: once more, there was an image on the film!

This time it looked like two ghostly figures standing alongside each other.

All of us, as they say, had mixed feelings. There was astonishment at the images appearing at all, curiosity as to what they meant, deep suspicion, a half-belief that something beyond that table might have produced the pictures, and a feverish desire to have another go.

We did have another go, but this time the table was distinctly tetchy, hostile even. During a quiet period we all heard a series of raps or creaks which did not come from the table, but from the area of the room behind George and between him and the green door. This series of light noises, similar to a stick being run along railings, was picked up by the tape-recorder. All the time this was happening the group was in contact, each person touching the hands of those on either side of him or her. I had my left leg up against George's right one and Saunders was similarly keeping tabs on his left arm and leg. He certainly never moved while the rapping went on. No other person in the group could have caused the rapping behind George and to my left, for my back was against the washing tank and Saunders' back was against the enlarger bench – there was no way round us.

After thirty or forty minutes we decided to break. George was asked to lift his left hand from the table and replace the camera lens-cap. We heard the rustle of his shirt sleeve. Then he gave a gasp. He cried out, 'The camera's not there!' Consternation.

George stood up in the dark and we heard him fumbling about. He discovered that the camera had been turned round 180 degrees on its panning-head and was facing diametrically away from the group into the corner by the green door. He replaced the lens cap and Dodo pulled on the light. The film in the camera was developed and proved to have nothing on it.

Both Saunders and I were deeply suspicious of George. We felt it was all to good to be true. But we tried by various means to eliminate some of our suspicions. The tapping noise we had heard from behind George had indeed been caused by the camera panning-head as it turned. From experimenting, we proved that even when the panning-head was locked you could *force* it to turn with creaking noises identical to the ones we had heard and which had been recorded. Nobody in the group could have turned the camera, so that left only two alternatives, (a) an accomplice, (b) some power not at present explicable. Since both George's workers (i.e. Rita and Ann) at that time were sitting round the table and had not moved, the accomplice would have had to be an outsider. I myself find the accomplice explanation an exceedingly difficult one to accept. I am prepared to believe that the force so often encountered in poltergeist cases was here responsible for the twisting round of the camera.

As to the photographs themselves, a number of interesting points are worth making. We started off with the premise that, on the face of it, we had taken two photographs in the dark and none of those present had seen any object which might have produced the two images. Was this in fact possible? Could an image appear on photographic emulsion emanating from a subject which would remain invisible to the human eye? The answer is yes.

The Kodak Research Laboratory was approached and gave us the following information: the human eye is only sensitive to that part of the Spectrum above infra-red and below ultra-violet, that is to say, the normal human eye can perceive Deep Red, Red, Orange, Yellow, Green, Blue/Green, Blue, Visible Violet. It seems that most panchromatic film emulsions, and especially Kodak-Plus-X, are sensitive to a part of the spectrum outside the visible range and extending well into the ultra-violet and possibly to the limit of glass lenses. Kodak told us that the sensitivity of plus-X emulsion ranges from Red 680 m/ Microns to Ultra-Violet 320 m/microns (possibly further). The range of human sight is roughly Deep Red (say 700 m/microns) to Visible Violet (400 m/microns). From this it is clear that images beyond 400 m/microns in the Ultra-violet part of the spectrum would be invisible to the eye but would be capable of appearing on film, but only if the camera lens was not itself a barrier to Ultra-violet light – some multi-element bloomed lenses do not pass Ultra-violet light at all.

So we decided to test the theory and George's camera. Bob Saunders was authorised to buy an Ultra-violet mercury arc lamp in a filtered envelope from Messrs Strand Electric and this was installed in the dark room at Buckell Hall. For readers technically minded, the lamp was a series choke fed and rated at 125 watts. When this lamp was switched on the dark room remained essentially dark to the human eye, though some materials were caused to fluoresce in the dark – white shirts, for instance, or white paper. With care in the choice of clothing and the removal of certain objects from the room a very good darkness level could be achieved. A series of photographs was taken under such conditions with a Kodak Retinette Camera (Schneider-Reomar lens), using Plus-X 35mm film at an aperture of f2.8 and an exposure of two seconds. The resulting pictures taken in what to the human eye was darkness, were clear and sharp and proved to our satisfaction that a low-level Ultra-violet image could be invisible to the human eye and yet appear on photographic film. In other words, the two images we had obtained did not represent a scientific impossibility, and provided the subject was there, the photographs did not have to transgress the normal laws of physics.

Further investigation of our photographs brought to light other interesting matter. There appeared to us to be a distinct relationship between the two prints. We were led to drop the theory that the second picture perhaps represented two figures standing side by side. In fact, we came to conclude that the subject of the second photograph was the *same* as that of the first at a different point in time.

Bob Saunders and I attempted to locate the subject in space at the time of the exposures. We came to the conclusion that a subject situated immediately over George's head was in the most likely position. This position immediately suggests a connection between George and the subject which I hesitate at this point to amplify. The developing story of the sittings needs to be further unfolded before we attempt such amplification.

The words 'spirit photography' have long been almost a synonym for fakery. Most people have produced 'ghosts' on their family snapshots by inadvertently double-exposing shots. A spirit photograph is the simplest thing in the world to produce. Traditional spirit photographs are almost without exception of the type where one image (the spirit) appears on top of another, the ground image being either a location or a person or persons. In one thing therefore, our two photographs are different: there is no suggestion of superimposition. If faked, the images were not procured by double-exposing the film.

If the photographs *were* fakes, there could be only one likely organiser of the faking and that was George. As a very skilful professional photographer he must be the immediate suspect. Let me speculate as to how a fraud might have been perpetrated. The negatives could have been prepared beforehand. They need not have been the two we saw put into or taken out of the camera, for a 'switch' could have been arranged by some sleight of hand. In our case, the photographs were essentially two of a group of three exposures, the third being a blank resulting from either no image to photograph, no tampered-with negative or the camera having been turned to the wall. How did the camera turn to the wall ? Either George was lying when he put up his hand in the dark and reported the camera not being there, and he then turned it himself, or an accomplice entered through the green door and turned the camera in our presence.

It is now nearly eight years since the night when the photographs appeared. My work has kept me in contact with George and his assistant Rita during those eight years and I have no reason to suspect either of them of not being scrupulously honest. I believe it impossible that George turned the camera on its tripod because we sitters heard no noise of this happening, but we *had* heard the clicks when George was seated with us and under control. I do not believe that an accomplice came in through the green door for in that tense ear-cocked atmosphere we would have heard some sound of the door handle, hinges, foot scrapings and fumbling – and these must also have been recorded: they were not.

It is a pity, of course, that we did not exercise a cast-iron control. I know I held George's wrists during the whole removal of the second and third negatives and their processing, so I am certain he could not have made a switch during that operation.

But that does not preclude the negative from the camera having been prepared beforehand. Still, in extenuation I may recall that it was Dodo's and my first attendance at a sitting and we certainly had not come prepared for anything dramatic ; did not, in fact, know that an attempt was to be made to take photographs. If George had intended to trick us by switching negatives, then my unexpected insistence on holding his wrists and keeping tabs in the processing room must have made a switch exceedingly difficult, if not impossible.

There I must leave the photographs for the moment, with the promise that I will return to the subject at the end of this chapter after further relevant happenings have been recorded : and at that time I will relate my own theories which, I hope, will provide at least a working hypothesis.

Our next sitting took place at Buckell Hall on 8 October 1965. Here is Bob Saunders' condensed report drawn up a day or two afterwards :

Present
    George
    Rita
    Ann
    Brian Branston
    Dodo Branston
    Bob Saunders
    Anne Whillock

Sitting held in small darkroom at Buckell Hall
Equipment
    MPP 5 x 4 plate camera
    Retina 35 mm miniature camera
    Plus-X film stock
    Philips tape recorder
    Mercury Arc Ultra-Violet light source 125 watts

Three exposures were made using Kodak Plus-X 5 x 4 plates – complete control was exercised by Mr Branston. All three negatives were unexposed and blank.

Several exposures were made on 35 mm film under UV

light – no unexplainable phenomena are present on the negatives although they demonstrate the effectiveness of invisible light photography in this kind of investigation.

During the sitting, cold draughts, smells and table turning were experienced, contact with 'George' was established – the text of the discussion is not reproduced here as it was somewhat laborious and the meaning almost a repetition of previous sittings.

During a period of 'communication' when the table was 'performing' quite well in total darkness it was decided to switch on the Ultra-Violet light to study its effect, if any, on the table movements – the table continued to rap intelligently as before – and so full room lighting was restored, the table continued to rap and a detailed study of the movements was made in very good light. With all hands removed movement stopped but commenced again when hands were placed lightly on or just above the surface of the table. The movements continued when (George) and I dropped out completely. At one point only Mr Branston's hands placed lightly on the table surface were necessary for table rocking to commence.

The phenomena were interesting and evidential and it was decided to arrange for a cine camera to be made available on future sittings.

Bob Saunders.

At the next sitting held on 15 October at Buckell Hall what appeared to be a typical mischievous Poltergeist phenomenon took place. The sitters were the same as the previous week with the exception of my secretary Anne Whillock who was not present. Bob Saunders reported:

Near the end of this sitting a message was received by table turning which intimated that the tape recording being made of the proceedings would be rendered useless.

When the lights were restored it was discovered that the microphone plug had been dislodged from its socket inside the tape recorder – all the tapes were blank. The machine had been started up at the beginning of the sitting before the room light was switched off, and a short test recording had been made and identified with the date – this recording was also missing proving that the microphone plug must have been dislodged before the session and the recorder were started. The microphone socket is actually inside the body of the recorder and it is unlikely that anyone (but myself) could have been responsible or even have known that the plug was loose or had been dislodged. The message telling us that the recording would be useless was received about four hours after the sitting commenced and I had actually recorded on both tracks of three and a half reels of tape.

The messages during the evening emanated from 'George' our regular communicant. The recurrent theme was: NO LOVE and NOBODY LOVES ME – and near the end of the session: NO CONTROL – TAPES USELESS.

Bob Saunders.

The pulling out of the microphone plug was enough to prevent recording and while being a typical poltergeist phenomenon could also have been done by a human hand. But what is more puzzling is that the test recording, complete with date, which Saunders had actually listened to at the start, had gone from the tape too! In the circumstances there is only one way this could have been achieved by human agency and that is by running that particular tape right back to the beginning. I own one of these Philips recorders myself and state from experience that it is impossible to operate the re-wind switch without causing a considerable click. Also because the re-wind is speedy, the tape gives an audible *whirr*. Apart from the rest of us having our attention caught, Saunders, who watches his gear like a hawk, would not have failed to notice.

The regular meetings at Buckell Hall continued for some weeks, being looked forward to by me with what the poet Gray calls 'a fearful joy'. I got the impression, once the sittings started, that we were frequently not alone. Often when the table began to move, it did so with great violence and made me, at least, apprehend that we were in close proximity to a tremendous power which, once free, would be impossible to control.

This is why the meetings were enjoyable. It is a human failing to want to run into frightful danger and to experience the exhilaration of having drawn back on the edge of the pit. We would sit for four or five hours often with little result, but rarely did a session finish without at least one startling phenomenon.

The group (less Anne Whillock) sat again on 29 October when we filmed the table rocking using my 16 mm Bell and Howell Casette camera. Since this sequence was in full light and I panned the camera all around and underneath, it was evident that nobody was moving the table in the ordinary sense. During a period with the lights out heavy breathing was recorded on the tape – without doubt from one of the circle. Messages were slow in coming though the table moved across the floor on request. Once the table asked WHY DO GHOST FRIGHTEN YOU ? Somebody said, 'But they don't.' The table said WE ARE LIKE YOU. A sitter asked 'Can we see you then ?' NO. 'Are you on film tonight ? NO. 'Was that you (i.e. "George") we had on the film last time? ' YES. 'Will you show yourself on the film again ?' NO . . . . PROOF . . . YOU WILL NEVER BELIEVE.

Before going on to describe a curious event during the course of this sitting I have to refer to a book I had been reading called *The Vital Sense* by H. G. Heine. On page 5 of the preface, Heine asserts that his book is 'an attempt to build a bridge between clairvoyance and other occult phenomena on the one hand and communication research on the other.' On page 3 of Chapter 1 he further asserts 'physiologists have located the archaic communication system which is responsible for the information we call clairvoyant and telepathic. The carriers of this information are the macrophages – amoeba-like cells in the body.' On page 84 Heine says 'eggs appear to have a stimulating effect on the macrophages, although the precise cause of this influence does not appear to be known at present.'

While being unconvinced by Heine's theories, I nevertheless was willing to give anything a go, so on this particular evening I had brought to the sitting a papier-maché carton holding half-a-dozen fresh eggs. I told nobody except Saunders and my wife why I had brought the eggs and simply put them down on the enlarger table where, for the early part of the session, they remained forgotten. I now report from the transcript of the meeting:

Mr Branston asked (George) to put the eggs on the table – the eggs were standing to the left of (George) on the enlarger platform (still in their container with the lid closed). (George) placed the box on the table with his left hand and the circle was resumed (this took place in complete darkness).

Almost at once the table began turning and by raps spelt: WATC ('Was that Watch ?') YES

EGG

Dodo Branston exclaimed 'WATCH EGGS!' and immediately a sound (which could have been the egg box lid opening) was heard; further table raps spelt:

LIG ('Light ?') YES

ON. 'Would you like the Ultra-Violet light on ? Would you like the mauve light on ?'

YES.

The U.V. light was switched on to reveal one egg missing from its place in the box – it was resting on the table about six inches from the vacant slot by the open lid.

Further table raps spelt: TRIC(L). 'Could we have the letter after C ?' K. TRICK.

'Is it possible for you to put the egg back in ?' NO.

'Will you put another out for us ?' (?)

IMOTHERE ('I am not here ?') YES (?)

YO ('You ?') YES WILN ('You will never ?') EA

LER ('Learn ?') YES

'You will never learn. What will we never learn ?'

No response.

I well remember the minor consternation this egg episode produced in the group. Because we switched on the Ultra-Violet light, the room remained to all intents and purposes dark, only the eggs and faces indicating their presence by fluorescing. Once again we suspected George. After all, he had handled the closed carton. At the time I was holding his right hand on the table and continued to do so. Bob Saunders allowed George's left hand to go free for no more than two seconds. If, during that time, he could shift the carton and open it noiselessly, squeezing it, extract one egg and rest it quietly on the table – then it was an extremely skilful conjuring trick. But why then didn't the free egg roll off the table ? For the table tipped at least one hundred and twenty eight times after the egg box had been placed on the table and before the light was switched on, during which period both of George's hands were controlled. At the same time, we would also have to accept that George was consciously manipulating the table to produce the message telling us to 'watch eggs' and 'switch light on.' It was very rum – and a typical poltergeist trick into to the bargain – and that, I believe, is the best explanation of it.

All these months, of course, George kept his photographic business going in spite of continued interference. After the meeting just reported, on the morning of 4 November 1965, a phone call to my office asked for someone to go to Buckell Hall because something odd had happened the previous night. Bob Saunders and I both went, taking a tape recorder. I quote from this recording made by George less than twelve hours after the experience he relates ; George said that he and Rita were both working late. During the evening of 3 November 1965 they had both 'experienced cold flowing feelings – in fact Rita felt it long before I did.' At about half past eleven, George was down in the darkroom working alone enlarging prints. He found he could not focus the machine, believed this was due to his being tired and went to get Rita from the front office to try her hand. She also found it difficult to focus, but at last they 'roughly got what he wanted' and Rita left the darkroom. In the meantime George reported :

I'd masked the safe light with a piece of card and put plenty of sellotape to hold it firmly in position. I was leaning over the enlarger and without any warning at all, I felt a terrific pressure around my neck at the back, almost as if some person or persons were gripping me in a vice-like grip. But being as I am quite strong, I found it impossible to move. It forced my head down as if someone had put both hands round the back of my head and was pushing me, trying to push my head right down till it hit the baseboard. I was resisting in an upward movement but it was impossible to do anything about it. Suddenly, it didn't push down any further but held me in such a position that I had to push the chair back with my bottom and struggle to get away, but found I could only pivot my body by my head ; and this must have happened for about 15 or 20 seconds. It wasn't my imagination, I know ; because one can generally feel pressure – a hand or a gloved hand. There was nobody else here but myself. And, as I say, it was impossible to move. And during this time I felt the energy leave my body at such a rapid rate that I thought if I didn't manage to get free soon, I was going to have a faint. It is the nearest – I have never fainted in my life yet – which is the nearest time I have ever fainted. My legs went weak, the whole of my body went weak. I think had it not been knowing subconsciously that there was some other form of life in here that I could go to, I would have collapsed.

Well, suddenly, as quickly as ... I felt suddenly gripped with this almighty sort of grip, this suddenly relaxed and disappeared. So I then made my way out of the darkroom and staggered to the other side and, by this time, I was quite frightened, and got to the other end where I told Rita about it ... but I had to sit down there for some time and then I would not come back into the (dark) room on my own. I waited for Rita to finish what she was doing and come down and give me some assistance. She, not having experienced any of this that I had gone through felt far more confident, and so made her way into the room, and she did make several observations, and one was looking at the thermometer. And we both read it together and it definitely showed just above 50 to 52 degrees – which is quite low considering that we had the heater in here, which normally holds the room at a temperature of 62, 65 and sometimes up to 70 degrees. This was actually at 11.35 p.m. . . . . . I did omit to tell you that just after the pressure was released and I was able to move once more, the card which was securely fixed by sellotape over the safe light was suddenly ripped down! It didn't fall down in the usual manner. It was quite definitely pulled down. You could hear the sellotape rip as it was pulled away and when Rita came back into the room, I staggered up the other end, as I said, earlier, and told her that something had held me firmly by the neck and I was unable to move, and I told her about the card having been ripped down from the safe light. And when she came into the room she saw the card hanging from the safe light ... There's no two ways about it: the sellotape hadn't melted. It was still sticky enough to re-stick the card back up and hold it quite firmly afterwards ... But after this ordeal and the safe light card was ripped off the safe light, we came down here again and carried on focusing many more of these things without any trouble at all, and they have now been accepted by the client ... It couldn't have been tiredness because after that we did another two hours work, and after that I drove another 15 or 16 miles over to Pinner and back again. And when I got home to relax at two o'clock in the morning, I read the newspaper in bed.

Neither Saunders nor I tried to guide George during his recorded account except for one question by Saunders towards the end, asking if he had cried out ? He said 'I couldn't speak. I was too scared ... I have heard of people being speechless, but I've never believed it, I've always thought that one could call out or do something. But quite frankly I could not while I was held call for any assistance at all.'

Perhaps an obvious explanation of what happened to George would be 'self-hypnosis,' 'auto-suggestion.' But the ripping off of the safe light card was objective enough. Even that could be explained away by the sceptic as being the result of the sticky tape losing its adherence through heat. Though George said he *heard* the noise of ripping. These happenings are such as can never be proven (or disproven) as objective occurrences. Though if they did happen objectively then they fit into the pattern of poltergeist phenomena.

At our next session (Buckell Hall 12 November 1965) there was what at first appeared to be a reference from our communicant 'George' to George the photographer's neck having been held:

Table:	I HOLD (Z) NECK
Rita:	Did you hold George's neck?
Table:	NO

A period of confused raps and questions from the sitters.

Table:	ME BEHI
Rita:	Me behind? was that 'George'?
Table:	YES.
Rita:	Behind who?
Table:	G . . .
George:	No! No! Oh Christ!
Table:	EOR . . .
Rita:	Is it George?
Table:	YES.
Rita:	Do you mean you're behind him now?
Table:	YES.
Brian:	Can we see you?
Table:	YES.
George:	I can't feel anything. Can we see you?
Table:	NO.
Rita:	Can we put the Ultra-Violet light on?
Table:	NO.
Rita:	How will we be able to see you, 'George'?
Table:	I HATE HIM.
Rita:	Why do you hate him, 'George'?
Table:	DEATH.
Rita:	Now 'George', we had a message like this before from you didn't we, about this?
George:	How about having the light on?
Rita:	Now 'George', you are trying to frighten our George, aren't you?
Table:	YES.

After further questioning the table intimated that 'George' was trying to frighten George because the latter had hidden something belonging to the communicant. However, no amount of questioning could elicit an answer as to what had been hidden.

At the next session (26 November) apparently 'George' was sulking and Susan, his presumed wife, took over communication. Little of interest came across apart from a reference to a book which I had been reading by Tom Lethbridge called ESP. 'Susan' said through the table that T. C. LETHBRIDGE's book (she got his initials right) was GOOD and that he was on the right lines. I had brought the book with me and was rather surprised when 'Susan' recommended it should be read from page 1 to page 148. When the lights were put on we found that page 148 was in fact the *last* page. Susan also intimated that she used to come to meetings at Buckell Hall longer than five years before but would not or could not say when.

'George', our sulky communicant, returned to the next sitting held at Buckell Hall in the darkroom on 10 December 1965. His attitude on this occasion was severe and sharp. The still camera had been set up as usual with the lens cap on and the shutter open. 'George' didn't like it and said through the table that though he would appear, it would not be on film. The table knocked and moved violently, getting hooked upon the enlarger table. Rita asked for the Ultra-violet lamp to be switched on and our George discovered that the still camera shutter had been closed. The UV light was switched off and George once more opened the camera shutter. The table again jammed against the enlarger. Dodo moved it away and it immediately jammed a third time. The following dialogue took place:

A sitter: All right. Leave it there, but give us a message. Did you close the shutter?

Table: I SAID NO FILM LIGHT DISOBEDIENT

Rita: Oh. We're very sorry about that, 'George'. We put the light on when he said no. Do you want us to close the shutter, or have you closed it? Do you want us to close the shutter on the camera? Do you not mind any more?

Table: YES.

Rita: Close then, George (the photographer) please.

George:	I'm not putting my hand out there!
Rita:	Brian, will you do it ?
Brian:	Yes, what do I do ?
George:	It's closed!
Brian:	I haven't touched it yet.

At this point the light was switched on and George said: 'He's done better than that! He wound it right on to the end of the film. You can't go from one frame to another unless it jams!'

Rita:	Did you wind the film through the camera ?
Table:	YES.
Rita:	Why didn't we hear it, 'George' ?

This question brought no reply. The table said NO when it was asked if another film could be put in the still camera ; it said NO when asked if I could use my movie camera. Then it repeated the word DISOBEDIENT and rapped out GREAT POWER ANGRE (Rita: 'Angry ?') YES. The table then, according to Anne Whillock's typed report, 'gets very agitated and cross ... moving very erratically all over the place. Tips over on its side on to floor.' There was an astonishing incident when George asked the table, ' "George", about three weeks ago you said that I covered up something of yours, or I hid something of yours. What did I hide?' No sooner was this said than the table rushed at George and knocked him off his chair!

After a lot of questions from the group, the table said that the hidden object was a newspaper and on being asked what year, from 1936 to 1942, gave a MAYBE for 1942.

Rita:	Was there something written in the paper that was important ?
Table:	YES.
Rita:	Was it about you, 'George' ?
Table:	YES.
Rita:	Can you tell us what was in the paper that we should know ?
Table:	DEAT
Rita:	Was it your death ?
Table:	YES.

Rita:	Was it in the obituary column?
Table:	NO.
Rita:	Was it a story?
Table:	YES.
Rita:	Was it an important headline?
Table:	YES.
Rita:	Were you murdered?
Table:	MAYBE
Rita:	Executed?
Table:	YES.
Rita:	And it was 1942?
Table:	MAYBE
Rita:	Why were you executed?
Table:	BAD
Rita:	You said you were not guilty. Were you guilty?
Table:	(No response)
Rita:	Do you think you were guilty?
Rita:	Did you do anything? (Away from the table there was a tapped YES). Is that 'Susan' tapping over there ?
Table:	YES.
Rita:	It's 'Susan' tapping over in the corner ? Well, she thought you were guilty ?
Table:	YES.

Further questions brought no response. At last the table rapped KITE WHERE WAS IT? Further questioning was interrupted by the tapped message EVIDEZ and Rita asked 'Was the last word 'Evidence'? *Table*: YES.

Ann:	Did you mean 'aeroplane' for kite, 'George'?
Table:	YES (very definite).

Further questioning allowed us to piece together the following story. A real aeroplane was the key to the mystery, a bomber – a big, English bomber. A friend of 'George' had been in the bomber which was lost on a mission. This friend could have proved 'George's' innocence at his trial. Apparently the friend's nickname was Taffy, a miner from the Rhondda Valley.

'George' said two other 'people' were with him, one his daughter, all apparently 'tied' to the hall:

Rita:	We'd like to find out who this other person is with you ? Apart from your daughter ?
Table:	GUIDE
Rita:	Girl guide ?
Table:	NO.
Rita:	Your guide from the 'other side' ?
Table:	YES.
Rita:	'George' – if we had a medium here, or one of us was mediumistic, you could come through your guide to us ?
Table:	YES (Very definite)
Rita:	Is there anyone here capable of doing this for you ?
Table:	YES.
Rita:	Will you spell the name? Would you like me to call the names out ?
Table:	NO.
Rita:	Spell the name, then? Are we even likely to be able to see you ?
Table:	YES.
Rita:	Well, which one of us do you want for a medium? How will we be able to . . .
Table:	(interrupting) NOT RE
Rita:	Not ready ?
Table:	YES.
Rita:	We're not ready ?
Table:	YES.
Rita:	How can we prepare ? . . .
Table:	BE BRAVE.
Rita:	We are being brave.
Dodo:	Are we ?
Table:	NO.
Dodo:	Who's not brave? Am I brave? NO. Is Brian brave? NO. Is George brave? NO. Is Bob brave? NO. Is Ann brave? NO. 'George', have you got

	faith in any of us particularly ? We're learning. We are coming close to you. Do you believe that ?
Table:	I TRIED G.S.
Rita:	George S? (the photographer). You frightened him, didn't you ?
Table:	YES.
Rita:	Well, if you try again you might not frighten him. But you held his head down, didn't you ?
Table:	YES.
Rita:	It's because we can't see you it's terribly frightening. Can we see you ?
Dodo:	Well, he says we are not brave enough. Are we brave enough ?
Table:	YES.
Dodo:	Are you afraid of frightening us ? Do you like him (our George) now ? He's not a bad chap.
Table:	NO.
Dodo:	You still don't like him?
Table:	NO.

The table rapped that the reason for dislike of our George arose from his having hidden the 'newspaper' and something else in addition more important than the newspaper but we couldn't find out what. Our communicant then ceased to communicate.

As I have said, our weekly sittings usually took place on a Friday night. Because the next Friday would be Christmas Eve we decided to sit on Wednesday 22 December. It turned out to be a memorable and shocking meeting.

The usual group gathered round the table in their usual positions in the dark room at about half-past eight. After quarter of an hour in the dark George yawned once or twice, and complained that he was tired. Rita said, 'I've had the most extraordinary feeling that something's been pressing up against my leg all evening.'

Dodo said, 'I've had a creeping all round my face . . .'

Ann: 'I always get a pain in my left arm before anything happens; and this happens every week – you can laugh if you want to . . . but I've had it this evening.'

After a time Dodo said, 'There's something tingling and funny in the side of my face, the back of my head – it's in me.'

George complained of feeling itchy, and Dodo said, 'You always itch, George, when it's coming.' Then she said 'We can hear a tapping – if it's someone tapping will you do "two" for "Yes" please ?'

The taps (wherever they came from) went twice.

Rita said, 'Well done! Can you tap on the table so we can all hear ?'

Dodo:	It sounds like someone far off.
Brian:	Is someone there ? I've got the pricklings.
Table:	Raps.
Dodo:	Oh good! At last! Good evening 'George' – is that you 'George'? You've been a long time contacting us ; haven't you got much power tonight ?
Table:	YES.

The table was asked to spell out a message but did not respond. After a time baby talk from the table suggested to Rita that the child 'Margaret' was attempting to communicate, but the table became violent as if a tussle for its possession was going on.

I said, 'I had a feeling that the table was moving differently from what we've had before, as though some different . . . was moving it.

Table:	G.P.K.
Rita:	Is that right ?
Table:	YES (Very definite).

PK is short for Psycho-Kinesis, and I remarked, 'Psycho-Kinesis means the movement of things without any apparent moving force. Are we going to see an example of PK tonight?'

Table:	YES.

Nothing much happened for a time, then we got some more apparent baby talk: O PETY WING which was interpreted (and accepted by the table) as O PRETTY RING, being thought to be a reference to Rita's newly purchased ring with a pearl and diamond cluster in the shape of a pentacle of five-pointed star.

The light was put on and Rita fetched the ring from the front office. It was placed in its box in the middle of the table. We probably hoped for a demonstration of PK in connection with the ring but even after considerable persuasion from the group nothing of the kind happened and 'Margaret' was at last asked to go and get her 'father'. Immediately. the table moved very violently and someone said, 'Hello George' in a placatory sort of way. The table still moved. But nothing of any value was recorded and the group had a break with the lights on.

The lights were switched off and after about fifteen minutes it seemed to me that my neighbour George was falling asleep. He did not reply when spoken to. At first this apparent slumber was taken lightly by the other sitters and Dodo suggested asking 'George' to wake him up. Someone else said. 'No. It might startle him.'

Suddenly, without any warning, a frightful scream, a terrifying screech ripped through the dark by my left ear and I felt George leap to his feet.

Because we were jammed together in a confined space with sharp metal and wooden edges protruding about us from the enlarger and its bench, from the washing trough, from the camera tripod, I was concerned that George would hurt himself and us. I stood up at once in the pitch dark and opened my arms wide in an attempt to catch him. At the same time I snapped over my right shoulder to Dodo my wife, 'Switch the light on!' I was pretty frightened. I found I had embraced something, and as the light came on I saw that I had hold of George's right arm under the armpit. His great head was close to mine, his wavy hair hanging heavy, his eyes open with the whites showing. Because he was heavy, all of seventeen stone, I couldn't support him long like that. In a flash I saw all the other members on their feet with their eyes starting out of their heads. I had to let George go slowly on to the floor, where he lay on his back with his left leg doubled under him at the knee. If he had been normally conscious, such a position must have been intensely painful for him. I asked Bob Saunders, who was standing by his right foot, to pull the left leg straight. He did so. Rita, who was extremely distressed, told Bob to go to the front office for a bottle of whiskey. He opened the door behind him and left. As I stood looking down at George, I thought at first that he had had an epileptic fit or a heart attack and I wondered if we hadn't killed him. Then I saw something quite extraordinary. I was staring at his face and there, standing straight up out of his left eye, which was half-open, was what appeared to be a pencil of cigarette smoke. It had the appearance of solidity and was about the length and thickness of a pencil, but grey and smoke-like. I was not the only one to see it, for Rita, who was standing at his feet in extreme agitation, weeping and wringing her hands, cried 'Look! He's steaming!' But it wasn't steam, and it wasn't cigarette or any other sort of smoke.

Everything was happening very quickly. George started to sing in a baby voice something like a nursery rhyme. My wife stepped over his body and as she knelt down by his shoulders I saw that the pencil of whatever it was had gone. Whether it went back into his head or dissipated outside, I don't know. Dodo began to rub his cheeks and chafe his wrists, trying to bring him back to himself. She became quite rough with him and I remonstrated, but then he started to struggle back to normality. Between us we got him into a chair, where he moaned and muttered and trembled as though he would shake his arms and legs off.

Measured by the recording we had made, George's seizure lasted from the time of the scream until he came to himself sitting in the chair for two and a half minutes. But the trembling continued for another two hours before he was sufficiently composed to drive home. He had no real recollection of what had happened to him. He tried to give us an idea, saying:

> I got the same feeling as when you go under gas. A feeling of sort of being taken away ... not going down a hole; the sort of feeling going into darkness. I don't remember what happened. I've never had that feeling before, anyway: A sort of feeling of being taken. You know, sometimes you feel faint, you feel as if you're falling? Well, it's *not* that sort of feeling. It's a sort of feeling as if you're moving backwards, but not away from anything, but the same time everything is

113

gradually diminishing: as if suddenly you are going to open your eyes and nothing is going to be there!

One thing came out quite clearly during the two hours in which he was trying to compose himself. George was never going to hold another sitting – nor at the time did we try to persuade him. We were all considerably shaken. But of course, Bob Saunders and I couldn't let matters rest there. During the days before and after the Christmas holiday the pair of us discussed what had happened. It seemed clear that George had gone into a trance and we had been caught completely unawares, even forgetting the danger we were putting him into by trying to bash him back to normality. Bob had not seen the 'pencil of smoke' phenomenon, having dashed out to get the whiskey bottle. I asked myself was it the end or the beginning of a 'materialisation'? I came to think that in spite of the suspect quality of ectoplasm, I had to believe my eyes and I *had* seen the phenomenon – and so had Rita. If it was ectoplasm, then did its appearance not have some light to throw on our two spirit photographs? Could their subjects have proceeded in some way from George? Saunders and I had calculated that if a real subject had appeared before the camera, its most likely position in space was immediately above George's head. Had the subject come in ectoplasmic form out of George's eyes, ears, mouth or nose? I think after seeing the 'pencil of cigarette smoke' phenomenon that this is just possible. However, the relationship between the two pictures would mean that the subject would have remained relatively in the same position in the room for perhaps half an hour or more including a period when the light was on and while George was in the processing room. After that, where did it disappear to? (For the third negative proved blank.) I am inclined to think that (if the pictures *are* genuine) there is another paranormal explanation which I will discuss later.

It was all very baffling, and as I have said, I was determined not to let the matter rest where it was. We just had to think of a means to persuade the reluctant George to go on.

5
The Reluctant Medium

After our last meeting in Buckell Hall on 22 December 1965, George was adamant that he would not sit again and run the risk of another trance. I was equally determined that we had to go on. If we didn't, then the work of the previous half year would be wasted. We were amateurs, I acknowledge ; we made mistakes, no doubt ; but when I reviewed what had happened I couldn't help believing that we might be on to something.

If one tries to assess the phenomena connected with the hall, most happenings appear to be of traditional poltergeist type : noises, knockings, footsteps, objects moving of their own accord, doors opening, lights going on and off, strange odours, cold spots. The evidence for some of the phenomena is uncorroborated, as for instance the floating oilcan; but on the principle of 'safety in numbers' which I put forward in the chapter on the poltergeist, I for one believe George's testimony and I believe the floating oilcan was an objective happening. Now, when things like that come within your ken you just can't ignore them, you *have* to try to explain them : at least, I have.

What, I think, was possibly unique in our relationship as a group with the Buckell Hall poltergeist, was that we entered into a dialogue (to use the current jargon) with it! People in the past have noticed that you could get answers from poltergeists, you could knock and they would reply : Virginia Campbell did it. In our case the 'dialogue' appeared to go on for weeks with the poltergeist acting and reacting to our current behaviour.

Now, in the past, poltergeist activity has been characterised by its haphazard quality ; but we were getting positive reactions in reply to something we had said or something we had done. I may list some of the more striking actions and reactions :

Action	*Reaction*
1. A medium is brought to Buckell Hall by representatives of the SPR and leaves his seat to investigate 'a sort of light on the wall.'	The table shoots across the room and forestalls the medium's intention by pinning him against a bench.[1]
2. At a sitting with SPR mediums 'Margaret' is asked to demonstrate that she is in fact present.	A stroking noise is heard on one microphone and the other crashes to the floor some six feet away from its original position.[2]
3. The group assumes the communicator to have been a murderer.	An outsider, Paul Bonner, is moved to write automatically 'I was not guilty.'[3]
4. The group sets up a still camera to test the possibility of taking photographs.	Twice an image appears on film. A third attempt to photograph is foiled by the camera being turned backwards 180 degrees on its tripod.[4]
5. The group arranges to record its sitting as usual on 15 October 1965.	The communicant intimates that nothing has been recorded and the microphone plug is found to have been removed from its socket in the recorder.[5]
6. The group is told to watch a box of eggs on the table.	When the lights are turned up, one egg has been taken from the box and placed on the table.[6]

[1] Page 65.
[2] Page 73.
[3] Page 83.
[4] Page 91ff.
[5] Page 98.
[6] Page 101.

7. The communicant orders NO FILM on 10 December 1965.	When the group persists with its still camera, the shutter is closed and the complete film wound through the camera although there is a mechanism in the camera designed to prevent the turning from one shot to the next before an exposure has in fact been made.[1]

Now it is firmly established that a poltergeist needs a focus through which to operate and that most often the focus is a young person, frequently female. In our case, the focus was indubitably George the photographer: George had turned out to be a poltergeist medium. Whether all poltergeist foci are mediums is a question I cannot answer, although one wonders when thinking (in this connection), of other trances as for instance those of Virginia Campbell. I think it is worth recalling that on the occasion when George went into his first trance Rita, Ann, my wife and I all complained of odd feelings. In fact, after George had been 'taken' and had come round, I find myself saying on the recording 'I'm certain that whatever it was, it was trying to get through each of us in turn, because immediately before it happened to George I got this feeling of coldness – pins and needles – and this is why I said 'there's somebody here'.[2] This raises an interesting question: was it chance that George became the medium and not any one of us others? Bob Saunders in his letter of 14 September to Miss Barrington (p. 87) had suspected Rita of mediumistic potential. It seems to me therefore, that one must consider the possibility of intervention by a third party to produce both poltergeist phenomena and messages through a medium, though at this stage I would not feel in a position to pursue this particular discussion.

It was baffling. And we just had to go on to get more

[1]Page 106.
[2]What I had actually said, according to the tape, was 'Is there someone there? I've got the pricklings.'

experience and more information. I suggested to Bob Saunders that we ought to seek the aid of the Society for Psychical Research and he got in touch with Medhurst.

George Medhurst was keenly interested in what had happened at our last sitting and, to cut a long story short, we enlisted his help in persuading our George to go on with the sittings. For myself, I wanted the proceedings to be conducted in full light so that we could film what happened, but Medhurst advised against this. He believed that nothing *would* happen except in the dark. I was willing to go along with this for a start, but determined to bring the sittings out into the light as soon as possible.

We had our first meeting of the new sessions on Friday 4 January 1966 in the darkroom at Buckell Hall. Our group was augmented by the addition of George Medhurst and we sat in a new order. Our George sat to the table in a deep leather chair with his back to the door leading into the small glazing room and kitchen. George Medhurst sat on his left, I sat on his right. Rita was next to George Medhurst and my wife was next to me. Ann and Bob took up the other places to form a circle.

The meeting was an alarming one for all of us except perhaps George Medhurst who had had long experience. The alarm came from our George's violence. We began with our hands on the table in the dark and, if the others shared my feeling, then it was again that of fearful joy, pleasurable anticipation of being frightened out of one's wits. Nor were we to be disappointed.

We were all sitting quietly in the pitch black when George jumped violently. He let out a startling shout and I felt the hair at the back of my head rise. I grasped his right hand with my left and the sitters formed a ring with linked hands. George began to groan, he rocked backwards and forwards – I could feel him moving in the dark. There was an extraordinary whistling sound, more grunts and groans and George Medhurst said: 'If you can understand me, will you please try to say "Yes"? Just the one word "Yes".'

> *George*:   Yes. Yes. Yes. Yes. Yes. Yes. Yes. Yes (*A Child's voice*?)

I found it increasingly difficult to restrain George and I have no doubt that George Medhurst was having the same struggle opposite me. Our George screamed loudly. He muttered a word which seemed to be 'water' stammeringly: 'W-W-Water.' There was whispering from him and unintelligible speech. He continued to struggle and eventually landed on the floor under the table.

At a later stage we began to suspect that wherever George was in his trance, he appeared to be in a wartime aircraft. He struggled violently and literally shouted in great excitement and agitation the following phrases and injunctions:

George: THE BLOODY HATCH, MAN, WON'T OPEN!
THE BLOODY HATCH!
THE BLOODY HATCH!
I TOLD YOU TO BREAK THE BLOODY HATCH!
GET BLOODY TAFFY OUT!
BLOODY TAFFY'S STUCK!
YOU SILLY BUGGER (*Strong regional accent*)
THE BLOODY HATCH! (*sounded like* BLUDDY HUTCH)
RUN! . . . I'M NOT A . . .
MEGAN!
MEGAN!

We broke up after midnight feeling rather shattered. Medhurst seemed satisfied and not unduly alarmed by the violent movements and struggles of George. We agreed to go on.

Next morning, a Saturday, I had an agitated telephone call from George. He described graphically something that had happened to him and which I got him to record the following Monday morning. I quote from the recording:

George: Quite frankly, I don't get anything out of this because I can't witness it. It's very much like inviting somebody along to a variety theatre, locking him in the lavatory, and at the end letting him out and saying, 'Well, did you enjoy that?' I've not seen a damn thing . . .

Rita: We could see you though – not your face, but your shirt (*Referring to a small amount of light from a torch*)

Brian: Well, when your legs went up we certainly saw that, at least. I was busy holding your arm, you see, and old Medhurst – every now and then he hit the ceiling when you threw him off. I mean, you were trying to get out of this – whatever it was.

Bob: The chair to you was an aeroplane and you just had to get out of it. And there was Brian and George Medhurst holding you in the very aeroplane you were trying to get out of.

Brian: But the one thing I remember seeing in this darkness was when your legs went up because Dodo gave me a nudge and said 'Look at his legs!'

Rita: But what about this business with the arms – trying to push up with the arms at one time, wasn't he? As though you were trying to push the hatch off, you see.

George: There's me, flying round at 20,000 feet trying to get out and you're all sitting drinking coffee . . .

Bob: George Medhurst was bubbling over when he 'phoned me and wanted to know if we were meeting next Friday.

George: Friday's inconvenient. Quite honestly, I must have a weekend free. If I felt as tired as I did this weekend – thank God I didn't have to come to work . . .

Brian: How *did* you feel after the night of the trance?

George: Well, absolutely utterly and completely worn out . . . One surprising thing that I found; (*Here follows an account of what he had already told me on the phone the previous Saturday morning*) on getting undressed to take a bath on Saturday morning I was most surprised to see a reddening of my skin, almost in the shape of a giant pair of braces ... it was about three inches in width and it extended from where one would normally expect to join a pair of trousers and across my back. The other thing was that I found that I had reddening between the legs ... obviously no braces could have made that mark because it was far too wide.

Brian: Where did these marks run ?

George: Well, down each side as a normal pair of braces would have done and then they – it went down in between my legs, almost like a harness, I should think or something like this. And in the centre of my stomach I had a round circle shape – probably a little larger than the bottom of an ordinary drinking glass, I should think; but this lasted somewhat to one o'clock in the afternoon. I found myself for the rest of morning peering under my shirt to see exactly whether the marks were getting more definite or not. But by about one o'clock they had ceased to show ...

Brian: Did these bands join anywhere ?

George: I couldn't say – short of standing on my head ! I couldn't say ; but it was noticeable when I stood in front of a mirror that I had these marks.

Brian: Did they go, the ones from your shoulders, straight down your sides, or did they appear to come together ?

George: Well, this is something I can't really say. I would have expected to see a band, like a belt band, round the middle. But I had nothing like this at all. But they did extend over my shoulders and ended up just below my shoulder blades.

Brian: How did you know this ?

George: Because I looked backwards at myself in the mirror to find out exactly where they did end.

Brian: And you can't account for them at all ?

George: No. Nothing at all. I was most surprised to see

Brian: Did they cause you any pain ?

George: No. Nothing at all. I don't know whether it was imagination but I felt the marks in between my legs here, and the skin felt sore. But I didn't know afterwards whether this was caused by some underclothing having sort of rucked up into a position that had caused a reddening of the skin. But it felt sore to the touch but not uncomfortable. But as I say, I feel nothing now.

Brian: Have you had anything like this happen to you before ?

George: ... Nothing like this has happened to me before.[1]

Bob: What about when you got home on Friday night ? Did you notice it at all then ?

George: No ; because I got undressed in the dark – I was ever so brave. It's been worrying me because all Saturday morning I was going like this (*peering in between his shirt and trousers*). Once or twice my mother said, 'I think you need a bath,' because I kept looking as if I had something down my shirt.

Bob: Point to the position of the 'round'.

George: I'll have to stand up, Bob. About there, just over the navel ... just a circular red patch.

Brian: I think we've got the point now. Would you connect that up with a parachute harness ?

George: Don't know. Never seen one, never worn one. I wouldn't know. Why ? Did I sort of float or something? Have I floated down from the roof or something? (*During his trance*)

Brian: We might as well tell you ...

Bob: I've got a note of what you said (during the trance), if you don't mind me telling you. You

[1]In fact, it had, though George himself did not know it. See page 78.

(Text above continues from top: them when I undressed and I was equally surprised to see that they had disappeared. The marks had disappeared because they were quite red.)

said, 'The bloody hatch won't open.'

George: Sounds a bit like me, shouting 'bloody this' and 'bloody that.'

Brian: But it was in a north country accent. It wasn't in your own accent.

Bob: In a Geordie accent. Then you said, 'I told you to break the bloody hatch.' Then you said, 'Get bloody Taffy out ... Bloody Taffy's stuck.' Then you looked at someone and you said, 'You silly bugger.'

George: Sounds a bit like me, doesn't it ?

Bob: Then you shouted again, 'The bloody hatch!' And then you shouted out 'Megan', which is a Welsh girl's name. The word 'hatch' led us to believe, it would seem, that you were in an aeroplane.

Brian: It ties up with this harness, you see.

Rita: Don't you remember the messages we had from 'George' on the table about Taffy ?[1]

Bob: The 'Kite' ? Remember – Taffy was a witness and was lost.

Rita: Well, that crash must have been after the murder. And Taffy went down and 'George' was saved, with the parachute.

Bob: The funny thing is the struggling with the hatch, you know, which you were doing. You were struggling to get through the hole.

George: Is that how I fell on the floor ?

Bob: You went through all the motions of baling out of an aeroplane.

Brian: And at one point you had your legs absolutely together, right up here, I mean, (*demonstrating*) higher than I can get them. They were going straight up.

Bob: Which is how a parachutist in fact falls, with his legs together like that – so they fall sideways.

George: Really! But parachutes wouldn't give you a mark, would they ?

[1]See page 108.

Brian: It depends – if you were caught on the lid, the hatch . . .

George: So in other words I can wear a paratrooper's tie, not having jumped ? 'When did you jump ?' 'Well, you're not going to believe this but I jumped out of a leather chair!' 'How far did you fall out ?' 'Eleven inches!'

Bob: Doesn't any of this ring a bell, George ?

George: Not a clue. Nothing . . .

Bob: Taffy went down with the ship. You were concerned about Taffy being stuck . . . and then out you went. And it all ties up with the 'kite' and Taffy being lost.

George: Well then, if I'm not Taffy, who am I ?

Brian: I don't think you're anything in this part. You're simply a means of recording what happened.

Rita: I think he was Taffy.

Bob: I think you were a person with Taffy.

George: So I'm not 'George' then ?

Bob: No, I don't think you could have been 'George' because 'George' said that Taffy went off and that was that.[1]

George: So, does that mean to say therefore, that we're haunted by somebody . . . ?

Bob: (*interrupting*) Who was connected with Taffy ?

George: And not by who we call 'George' ?

Rita: Well – he can have any name.

George: Or does it mean to say then, that we're haunted by the whole crew ?

Rita: My theory is this: that he was in the plane with Taffy and whatever has happened – this murder business – had happened before that flight, when Taffy was with him . . . .

Bob: (*interrupting*) But the murderer[2] was an AC2 – ground staff – he wouldn't have been in an aero-

[1]See page 108.
[2]I.e. Koopman.

124

plane, so you couldn't have been 'George' – if 'George' is the so-called murderer, then he would never have got off the ground, so you were someone else, I'm afraid in the plane with Taffy: a north country chap from Newcastle!

It is practically impossible for a reasonable person to believe that George's trance utterances were any other than words and situations dredged up from his own sub-conscious mind. It is not easy to believe his story of the parachute harness, a story uncorroborated by anyone else. For myself, I do believe it, partly because stigmata had appeared on his body before without his apparently noticing (the scratch marks on his cheek, see page 78), but mainly because I was to see other stigmata appear on his body virtually before my very eyes. I may make one point: when we described the marks to a Battle of Britain pilot, he had no difficulty in recognizing the old war time D-type parachute harness no longer in use.

It took some six weeks before we were able to bring about the right conditions for a ciné filming session of George's trances with full lights. This occurred on 18 February 1966, and we moved from the darkroom into the large studio. Those present were George, Rita, Ann, George Medhurst and a friend, John Styles, Julian Baldwin, a BBC sound recordist, Bob Saunders and myself. Bob was to work the camera while Julian recorded the synchronous sound. The proceedings were filmed with a sync Auricon 16 mm camera running at 25 frames per second and a Nagra tape recorder with mains pulse injection. The lighting was set up to give minimum exposure at f2.8 and we exposed 1,600 feet (in two rolls) of Ilford Mark V film rated at 400 ASA. This was later processed by Kays Laboratories whose negative report was Roll 1 printer light 8/10; Roll 2 11 – O.K.

The Auricon camera was particularly suitable because it could take a roll of film one thousand feet long; this, if necessary, would give us a continuous running time of nearly half an hour. The other two commonly used professional 16 mm cameras, the Arriflex and the Eclair, would have given only 10 minutes continuous running. The Auricon camera is fitted with a door which takes up the whole of one side of the camera body. While we were setting-up, I noticed that the camera door was slightly ajar and I called Bob Saunders' attention to this. He told me that he had previously secured it by means of its large thumbscrew. Later, when the pair of us were adjusting one of the camera tripod legs Bob noticed an event which he wrote down shortly afterwards as follows:

I quite clearly saw a hand quickly unscrew the latch again. The effect of an open camera door would have resulted in complete 'fogging' of the film. I am not sure exactly how I managed to see the hand unscrew the latch because the camera was between it and my direct line of vision, but the camera door was certainly ajar when I checked it afterwards. George was standing in the vicinity at the time and could have been responsible although I personally doubt that it was a conscious action.

The sitting began with the group forming a horseshoe shape, George at the toe of the horseshoe, George Medhurst holding his left hand, I holding his right and the other sitters (less Bob and Julian) down each side. The camera, with Bob behind it and Julian with his recorder behind Bob, faced directly on to George.

At first it looked as though our attempt at filming a trance was going to end in failure for the simple reason that George could not or would not 'go off.' The sitting had begun at about 9.30 pm and for 40 minutes nothing abnormal happened.

I then suggested that we should create our own darkness, a subjective darkness, by shutting our eyes. In a very short time we others were startled into opening them again for George gave a sudden jump and went into a trance. He struggled, sometimes violently, groaned as if in pain, shouted loudly and he and Medhurst exchanged words as follows (I quote from the film sound):

George: It . . . it's hot . . . it's hot.
Medhurst: Yes. Where are you?

George: Here. Over here.

Medhurst: Where ? Tell me just where you were.

George: It'll be dawn in another hour. It's going to be hot. It's going to be hot.

Medhurst: What day is it ? Be still, be still, be still. Be calm!

George: T ... Tu ... Tu ... Tuesday!

Medhurst: What day of the month ?

George: Tue ... (*very loudly*) TUESDAY! Tuesday! .... They'll be coming 'ome soon ... It's going to be hot.

Medhurst: Relax. Tell me what year it is ... The year.

George: You ... you know ... you know ... For ... For ... For ... Fort ... Forty ... the .. th ...

Medhurst: Three ?

George: Th-three.

Medhurst: Three ?

George: Yes.

Medhurst: Forty-three ?

George: TUESDAY! (*with considerable violence*). The grass is damp. The grass is damp. She's standing over there. She is standing ... service. Service. Service.

Medhurst: What service ?

George: Service ... F ... F ... Failure ... Failure ... Failure ... Rear ... Fail ... Failure on the rear ... You've come to see ?

Medhurst: Tell me where you are. Are you on the ground ? Are you lying on the grass ?

George: Standing! ... You can see!

Medhurst: What is your name ?

George: He'll frighten all the bloody cows again when he comes in! (*Laughs loudly*) Henderson always comes low! (*Laughs*).

Medhurst: Tell me your name.

George: (*Shouting*) BIGGS! .. I can hear them! Service on the rear.

Medhurst: Where do you think you are now ?
George: On the station.
Medhurst: What station ?
George: Can't tell you. No names to be given! It'll be dawn soon. It's getting hot now. It's going to be hot today. Very hot!
Medhurst: Can you hear me ?
George: You've come to look ?
You've come to see her have yer ? To check her ?
Medhurst: To check what ?
George: The rear.
Medhurst: What's wrong with the rear ?
George: Sick. The usual.
Medhurst: What is the usual ? Tell me.
George: You know. The usual. She's jammed.
Medhurst: And what usually happens ?
George: I'm ill! Sick. (*Very loudly*) SICK!
Medhurst: Lie back and be still. What are you trying to say ? Be calm!
George: (*Weeping and upset*) It's jammed again! They all jam! (*shouted words here which are unintelligible but sound like:*) SNGUU DAM!
Medhurst: This was a long time ago –
George: It's jammed!
Medhurst: – and you're remembering –
George: NO!.. P-ninety two four always sticks!
Medhurst: Lie back! This was a long time ago!
George: Can't see her. Stuck! It's stuck! It's the sixth that's stuck! The sixth!
Medhurst: This was a long time ago!
George: ... See it now! I can see it now! Come and look!.. See it! I can see it! It's stuck now!
Medhurst: This was many years ago –
George: Service. Service. Stick. It's stuck! The rear. Hy ... hy ... hydraulic ... hydraulic failure (*straining*) hy ... draulic ... It's stuck! STUCK!

	STUCK! S ... S ... Service. Service, service, service. P nine two four ... rear, the rear, the rear!
Medhurst:	Who else is there ?.. Whereabouts is that ?
George:	F ... f ... Waiting, waiting, come.
Medhurst:	Waiting for what ?
George:	The first back.
Medhurst:	This was a long time ago.
*George*H	F ... f ... Fred ... Fred ... Fred ... I checked. I checked the rear. I checked the rear, Fred! I checked the rear, Fred! I checked, Fred!
Medhurst:	Be quite calm.
George:	I signed, Fred! I checked. His mother. Fred ... Fail ... fail ... FAILURE! (*shouting*) P NINE TWO FON (*phonetic spelling*). It's not long past! Past! A ... arrival. Checked! Checked! Fred.
Medhurst:	Who is Fred ?
George:	Flight s ... s ... (*very loudly*) FRY!
Medhurst:	I want you to wake up, George S——.
George:	(*shouting*) MY ARM! MY ARM! BARBED WIRE! BARBED WIRE! (*Groaning*) My arm, my arm, my arm, Oh my arm!

Before I comment on this trance, which we filmed 'sync' and from whose sound track I have copied the words, I want to describe its extraordinary finale. George broke away from my grasp momentarily and gripped his left arm as though he had experienced a sudden sharp pain. My curiosity to see what had happened to his arm was intense and I asked Rita to help me slip his jacket off and roll back his shirt sleeve. At this time he was coming out of trance but by no means himself again. I was astounded to see six great scratches criss-crossed over the skin running from just below the shoulder. Rita and I looked at each other in amazement and I told her to roll his sleeve down quickly before George came round and saw the marks himself. When he did come round, and with the camera still running I asked him what, if anything, he remembered of his trance. He

E*

said he remembered nothing. Have you got a pain in your left arm ? He rubbed it and said no. Can you explain why you thought towards the end of your trance that you had a pain there ? Only because if I was struggling you may have wrenched me. I asked him to roll his sleeve back and look. When he saw the scratches – they varied from 3 to 6 inches long and to my eyes seemed to have got redder and angrier (Rita confirms this) – his eyes popped out of his head. I taxed him with having faked the scratches. He denied it strenuously. I now quote from Bob Saunders' report made soon after the happening:

> Brian Branston deliberately scratched himself in the same area with a pin in an effort to simulate the markings, but the scratches were thin and the skin broken. (George's) marks looked something like 'cat' scratches ... The markings were raised pink, and criss-crossed but the skin was not broken ... (Rita) told me that the scratches were only just visible when she first examined them immediately after the trance. (Ann) noticed that (George) did not have any scratches on the arm at 5 o'clock on the same day (she had been processing with him and his shirt sleeves were rolled up) ... It was in my opinion remarkably consistent with the evidence, i.e. that 'Biggs' brushed against a barbed wire fence.

I have no doubt in my own mind that the scratches come into the category of genuine stigmata. They were produced psychosomatically by George's unconscious mind and mirrored an event through which he had lived in his trance. There is enough internal evidence in the 'speeches' to reconstruct that event tolerably well.

George was speaking in the character of an aircraft technician whom he called Biggs. The year was 1943, it was a Tuesday before dawn in high summer and the grass was drenched with dew. The place was a war time bomber air station somewhere in the country with cows grazing in the fields and 'Biggs' was preoccupied with two events. The first was a hydraulic rear failure in an aircraft standing nearby which he named 'P Ninety two four' and the second was the return of bombers which had been on a night raid. He was frantic to justify his workmanship to a flight (Sergeant ?) Fred Fry, and one of the pilots expected back was called Henderson.

After the weekend I set out to check the hard evidence accruing from George's trance. There were three names and what appeared to be an aircraft number. I got nowhere with the men's names, but the BBC Reference Library did track down the mysterious 'P Ninety-two'. Only one aircraft ever had been given that designation. I quote from the magazine *Flight* dated 13 June 1946:

TURRET FIGHTER. A Boulton Paul Project of 1939/40 20-mm Guns in Low-drag Turret ... The P92, as the projected fighter was designated, was to seat a crew of three – pilot, navigator and gunner – and was to have a range with auxiliary tankage of 2,000 miles. A half scale model with two Gipsy engines was built and flown extensively, but soon after work on the full-scale prototype was started it was decided to transfer all design activities to turrets.

In his trance George had referred once to a 'P Ninety two four' and once to 'P Nine two fon.' The official designation of the aircraft (as far as I could find out) was never 'P Ninety two four', for the full scale prototype was called 'P 92' though the half scale flying model *was* named 'P 92/2'. George's 'four' may well have come from the gun turret which the *Flight* article already quoted named the 'Boulton Paul 4 – Browning turret.' A further reference in *Flight* 8 July 1955 to the P 92/2 gave the information that 'a half-scale model ... the P 92/2 was built by Heston Aircraft Ltd. and extensively flown.' The contract number was B. 29037/39; it was 'taken on charge, 29-8-41, struck off charge 20-11-45'.

Judging from these dates, the aircraft should have been undergoing tests in 1943, the date mentioned in George's trance. Further interesting details from the two *Flight* articles are that the body of the aircraft was a wooden one 'of plywood monocoque construction throughout,' and the test pilot was named Flt Lt Feather. It may be significant that the accommodation for the pilot in the half scale model was extremely cramped and his escape in an emergency would have been difficult: 'Heston Aircraft were unable to obtain a half-scale pilot ... means had to be found of providing the pilot with necessary emergency egress. This problem was solved with the help of a single control which simultaneously released a large fuselage panel[1] and collapsed the pilot's back rest. Had it been necessary for him to bale out, he would have fallen backwards and then rolled and wriggled his way sideways out of the aircraft' *Flight* 20 June 1946.

I phoned the Heston Aircraft Company (now called Hestair) and asked to speak to someone who knew of the P 92/2. My informant, Mr Dowden, the works manager, told me that he knew of no one called Henderson or Fry who might have been connected with the plane. 'What about Biggs?' I asked. 'Oh yes,' he said, 'Reg. Biggs, the carpenter. He was the foreman in charge of wooden aircraft production.' Mr Dowden had worked for the Heston Aircraft Co. and Hestair for over thirty years and knew Biggs personally. He told me Mr Biggs had left to work for the John Compton Organ Company in Greenford. When I enquired there, I found he had retired in 1965 and was given his home address.

When I discussed my findings with Bob Saunders, we both expressed surprise that Mr Biggs should still be alive: one somehow expects communicants or characters playing parts in a medium's trances to have 'passed over.' I now quote from Bob Saunders' report of his search for Mr Biggs made just one week after George's trance and in fact, as soon as I had collected information on the aircraft:

On Friday 25 February I met Mr Biggs. I was immediately struck by his resemblance to the 'spook' photograph taken in Buckell Hall some few months ago, in particular his nose, mouth and hair were remarkably similar in detail. Mr Biggs informed me that he worked for Comper Aircraft at Heston (the original name of Hestair) from 1930 to 1938! He knew nothing of the P.92 project. He actually worked on small aircraft of the civil 'King's Cup' class and was concerned

[1]George's 'hatch' of his trance of 4 January 1966, see page 119.

with a secret project for Fairy Aviation called the 'Mouse'. He joined John Compton Organs in 1946 and retired in 1965 ... I read the transcript of the seance to Biggs under the pretence that it was an extract from a book written by (George). He made no comment but I felt at the time that it *might* possibly mean something to him. He said afterwards, 'How did you get on to me ?' Mr Biggs had never heard of (George).

For his part, George had never heard of Reginald Biggs, but there is one occasion when their paths, unknown to both of them, may have crossed. Shortly before Biggs retired from John Compton's, George was called to their Greenford factory to photograph one of their organs. At that time, both he and Biggs were probably for a space under the one roof.

We continued our meetings, occasionally missing one week when people had to be away or some other reason made it inconvenient. Without fail, when we did meet, George would go into a trance and we would film it. Because at first we did not have a 'budget' for our film, the BBC personnel gave their services free and so we used different technicians according to their availability. I remember one Friday night when our recordist was, for the first time, Ron Edmonds. We were filming in the large studio inside a corner 'set' made with two flats at right angles. Ron and his recording gear were placed behind the camera outside the set and in the shadows. The interior of the set was brilliantly lit with film lights but the remainder of the studio was dark. During a break in the filming, George just having come out of a trance, there was a loud crashing noise at the other end of the studio near the office. We were all startled, because there was nobody there. Someone said, 'Ron, go and see what that was, please.' As I say, it was Ron Edmonds' first attendance and George's trance state had already shaken him somewhat, so he was rather slow in getting to his feet to venture into the shadows. As the person in a position of overall responsibility, I felt he ought not to be coerced and (although I admit to being nervous) I said, 'It's all right, Ron ; I'll go.'

I walked out of the brightly lit set, strode over the camera cable, film boxes and Ron's recorder and turned into the darkness. I took two strides towards the far end of the hall and suddenly had the sensation of walking through what I can only describe as a 'force field.' In other words, I seemed to walk into an invisible curtain beyond which was a continuing condition which was quite different from the filming end of the hall. If I say that it was almost like having mild 'pins and needles' over the whole of one's body, then a sceptical reader must inevitably say, 'That's all it was'. There's just this one puzzling difference. After I had discovered nothing which might have caused the crashing noise and walked back towards the set, the 'pins and needles' disappeared instantly as I walked over the spot where I had first felt them. One doubts one's senses on such occasions and I said nothing to the others at the time. Of course, to prove that the experience was not subjective I ought to have asked another of the party to walk down the hall. But I didn't.

We filmed a remarkable trance session during which a struggling George, with George Medhurst and John Styles holding him down in a leather armchair, appeared once again to be on the RAF tack.

The following interchanges took place, interchanges which as they happened I found difficult to understand ; but as all the information emerged, the meaning became clear. To save the reader puzzling, I have occasionally put an explanatory word in brackets, otherwise the record is exactly as it was filmed and recorded :

George:	Leave, leave, leave! (*I thought at first he was asking someone to leave, but in fact he was referring to a serviceman's leave*)
Medhurst:	Leave, yes.
George:	(*Struggling to speak*) Se – se – se ('*Seven*')
Medhurst:	Yes.
George:	Se –
Medhurst:	Yes. Try to speak.

George: Pass. (Gasping) Pas – ass ('*leave pass*')
Medhurst: Yes. What about it ? Yes.
George: Leave.
Medhurst: Yes, yes, now what about it ?
George: Leave.
Medhurst: Yes, yes. Try to say more about it. Try to say
               more about it.
George: Pass.
Medhurst: Yes.
George: Se – se – se – seven – ty – ty – t –
Medhurst: Yes
George: – ty – ty
Medhurst: Seven
George: – ty – ty
Medhurst: Seven what ?
George: – ty – two

So far we had got 'leave pass, seventy-two.' At this stage George got his left hand free from Medhurst's grasp and although Medhurst and I still held his wrist, George managed to point across his body towards something which appeared to be near him on his right. In order to further the action (if possible) because by now George was attempting to feel or stroke whatever he could see, I said loudly 'You've got it!'

Medhurst: Now what is it ? What is it ? (*As far as we were
               able to see George was gesturing to an empty
               armchair*)
George: HIM!
Medhurst: Who? Who is it? Yes. Who is it? Who is it?
               Is somebody there?
George: Him! HIM!
Medhurst: Who ?
Brian: Tell his name!
George: A – a – ah!

The whole of George's attention was on what to us was an empty chair, though I must confess to hoping that the film might be picking something up. George stretched his right leg and hooked his foot round the chair leg and dragged it towards him. I said, 'Now, you've touched him. Speak his name.' Suddenly, with a great paroxysm of vocal and physical exertion, George literally screamed 'HE'S DEAD! HE'S DEAD!' and in trying to contain him, John Styles, Medhurst and I were all pulled on to the floor on top of George and his own upset chair. For a few seconds he lay on the ground and Bob Saunders, working the camera, zoomed into a big close-up of his head. When I looked at the pictures later on, I was a bit surprised in view of what now follows to see a hank of rope reminiscent of the hangman's rope one sees in western films (about which we knew nothing at all). We pulled the chair back on to its feet and dragged George, still entranced, into it. He raised his right hand straight above his head with the forefinger pointing up and said in a stern voice, 'You will be taken from this place...,' Then in a voice filled with concern he whispered, 'Mistake.'

Medhurst: Mistake ? Whose mistake ?
Brian: And what will happen ?
Medhurst: Still now. Be still. Stay still.
Brian: Say what will happen.

But George said no more. He slowly came to himself, but not before he had freed one hand and put it up to his throat. At the same time he lifted both legs held firmly together off the ground. When he did come round, George went to tidy up in the dressing room but quickly came rushing back to us in the studio when the following conversation took place (quoted from the film):

Brian: Since you came out of trance you had a chance of going into the dressing room and tidying up. You came rushing out of there in some trepidation. Why ?
George: Well, only because I find now that I have a mark round my throat which I believe has been caused by my tie being too tight.
Brian: May we see that ?
George: Yes. Sure. Do you want me to take my tie off ?

Brian: Yes please. How far does it go round ?
George: I don't know. I haven't seen the back yet. But
             I'll turn for you. (*He turned a full circle on his
             chair and we filmed the mark. It was about the
             width of a finger, extremely regular, red in
             appearance and went completely round his neck
             unbroken*)
Brian: And how do you think it came there ?
George: Well, only because my tie's been too tight, I
             think.

I myself have no doubt that George had once more unconsciously produced stigmata. The explanation he gave was
his conscious mind's defence against believing a phenomenon
which was enough to 'blow' any ordinary person's conscious
mind. It all fitted in with the scene of which in his trance he had
been a part. Mainly he appears to have been the judge in a
murder trial and to have seen (presumably) the accused who
was eventually hanged, for he cried 'He's dead! He's dead!'
The opening of the trance with its information about a seventy-
two hour leave pass connects up with the real Aircraftman
Koopman who was condemned for committing the murder of
Mrs Brewer and her baby daughter while on a seventy-two hour
leave pass from his unit.

Bob Saunders and I were very curious to view that particular
batch of film rushes hoping we might see something or someone
sitting in the empty chair. But there was nothing on the film –
perhaps because the film we were using, Mark V, was not
sensitive to ultra-violet emanations ; or, as the sceptical have
every right to say, because there was just nothing there.

That George saw someone, I have no doubt whatsoever. He
could not tell us who it was because the percipient had been
his unconscious mind. I do not believe, because George could
not remember when conscious and because we others had seen
nothing, that it is against the law of physics that something or
somebody could have been there. We ordinary folk receive our
impressions of the world outside us through our five senses –

sight, hearing, touch, taste and smell. The immediate sense impressions are filtered through a sense organ, the eye, the ear, taste buds and so on. But what the eye sees is not the picture. Our sense organs have definite limitations. In modern town man (for example) the sense of smell has atrophied to such an extent that he is lucky if he can distinguish between 'nice' and 'nasty' smells. The sense of taste is perhaps not quite so limited, we can appreciate sweetness, bitterness, saltiness, acid, alkali, we know what tastes 'nice' or 'nasty' – but having said that, you've said all. Then take touch – we can differentiate (not always) between hot and cold, hard and soft, smooth and rough, but not much else. A local anaesthetic will easily do away with any sense of touch ; just as a rare type of hereditary disease deprives its victim of any feeling of pain. A general anaesthetic will knock out all the areas in the brain deputed to interpret the stimuli coming from the sense organs.

We know already that the sense organs when working normally only do so between limits. The human eye can accept and deal with light waves between ultra-violet and infra-red and not outside that band. The normal human ear can cope with sound between 10 and 100 decibels – not softer or louder (without pain).

But the sense organs are useless without that area in the brain which translates their stimuli into sounds or pictures etc. On the other hand we know that a human being can *see* without a stimulus having come via the accepted organ of sight, the eye The simplest example of seeing without the use of the eyes is during dreaming. And at the present time experiments are being conducted to produce pictures in the brain of blind people using electrical stimuli. What nobody can say for certain is whether the brain does actually auto-stimulate to produce dream pictures, or whether some outside stimulus has to be applied even though it may not come via the eye.

Having said this, I see nothing logically impossible in a subject being perceived in picture form directly by the brain without having to pass through the filter of the eye. One can then theorise that the subject may be viewable by one person though not by another. In this way, it would be possible for George to see a subject which we others could not ; in this way it would be possible for one person to see a ghost and another not – while both could be seeing the same 'background'. It is rather like a double-exposure in film terms : two people are seeing the same subject via the eye, but one of them is also seeing an additional subject via stimuli which by-pass the eye and work only on the brain.

The Friday night meetings at Buckell Hall were beginning to tell on all of us. George was becoming more and more reluctant to go on and I believe I am right in saying that there was a general impression of our being plugged in to a power which wasn't altogether benign. In a way, we were like explorers who have penetrated into country unknown to them, a country which seemed vaguely hostile. I began to get the idea that we should soon have to turn back. However, before we did so we were vouchsafed other wonders, the telling of which, when we did return to habitable land, made reasonable people look askance at our travellers' tales.

At one of our last sittings there was a remarkable change. Up to this time (it was in April 1966) George had been like an actor through whose mouth words had conjured up situations in which we were aware of other 'characters' taking part. There was, for instance, the bomber station scene with at least three other people, Biggs, Henderson and Fred Fry ; there was the crashing aircraft scene with Taffy and others ; there was the courtroom scene with a judge and 'him.' All these scenes appeared to be linked together in a way which I shall discuss later.[1] The new development was quite different : there was no link with aircraft and, most striking of all, George suddenly developed into what I can best call the traditional type of medium by manifesting a 'control.'

A control or guide is the traditional medium's channel between this world and the next. Red Indian Chiefs, Chinamen with squeaky voices, doctors of medicine appear to be very popular controls. For many people who find it hard to credit

[1]See page 145.

them, they pop up like pantomime clowns as figures of fun, products of the medium's unconscious phantasy. I must say that George's control, when she suddenly appeared, made me want to laugh. She spoke in a high falsetto voice and eventually gave her name.

Medhurst: Tell us your name. What is your name?

George: (*In a high falsetto voice throughout*) You have no communication with this man (*Presumably George*).

Medhurst: Who is speaking now?

George: You know not of me.

Medhurst: Yes. Tell me please, who are you?

George: This man has now passed to our forcefield.

Medhurst: Yes. Which man are you speaking of? Are you speaking of the medium?

George: *You* call him a medium.

Medhurst: Yes. Is he not a medium? I'm speaking to you now, not to the medium. Tell me about yourself.

George: It is you that use the word 'medium.'

Medhurst: What name should I use?

George: 'Septella.'

Medhurst: 'Septella?' What is that name? Is that your name? I don't quite understand.

George: This man's heart is beating fast.

Medhurst: That's not a thing to be alarmed about.

George: (*Grunts*).

Medhurst: Who is this now? Try to speak if you can. We are anxious to keep in touch with you.

George: What is it you require?

Medhurst: Now I don't want to bring him back (*the 'him' being the violent communicator*) but I want to know about the violent entity who was apparently controlling what I was calling the medium last time and on other previous occasions. I want to know who that entity is?

140

	And I want you to tell me what you can about him.
George:	This is outside my forcefield.
Medhurst:	I see. So you are not aware of events outside your forcefield ?
George:	I am not aware of things that happen here ... (*For a long time there was verbal sparring between Medhurst and the control who had still not revealed a name, and we did not seem to be getting much forrarder. Then the following exchanges took place*:)
Medhurst:	There have been some disturbances here that have worried the people here.
George:	(*Still falsetto*) I know of these.
Medhurst:	Are you responsible for these ?
George:	I am *not*.
Medhurst:	Do you know who or what is producing this disturbance ?
George:	Of course.
Medhurst:	One of our reasons for making these experiments is to try to remove this disturbance, because it worries and upsets the people here. Can you help us ?
George:	There is no need for worry. It is because you don't understand. (*A sort of rivalry for control of George seemed to develop between the falsetto voice and Medhurst and the communicant apparently decided to give a demonstration of power*:)
Medhurst:	What's happening now ?
George:	I will control his arm (*George freed his right wrist from my grasp and raised his arm stiff as a poker above his head*).
Medhurst:	May we try to pull it down to see how far it's controlled ?
George:	You may try to ask him to lower it.
Brian:	Will you lower your arm? (*Arm stays upright*)

141

Medhurst:	Could we physically pull it down?
George:	You will find that he resists. (*I stood up and gripped his wrist with both hands and pulled. The arm stayed upright. I dare say if I had exerted all my strength I could have pulled him out of his chair but I doubt whether his arm would have moved in relationship to his body. But because we wanted some spectacular manifestation I said in a flattering way:*)
Brian:	You are stronger than we are. You are stronger than we are. Now put it down yourself. (*No change*)
Medhurst:	I take it that you can keep it up indefinitely ?
George:	I can do anything with this man.
Medhurst:	Why are you making this demonstration ?
George:	To prove to you that you know very little.
Medhurst:	In what way does this prove ?
George:	You do not *control*! This man cannot be controlled until he was passed back.
	(*After a while George began to groan and Medhurst asked 'What's happening now ?'*)
George:	(*falsetto*) I'm talking to him.
Medhurst:	What are y –
George:	(*interrupting with startling shout*) ALFREDA!
Medhurst:	Who is this ? Who is this ?
George:	(*quietly falsetto*) I think that he fears my presence.
Medhurst:	What did he say ?
George:	He calls my name.
Medhurst:	Oh, will you repeat your name please, in your own words ?
George:	ALFREDA!
Medhurst:	'Alfreda' – that's why you smiled, earlier when I asked if you were alive ?
George:	There is no need to hold his arm (*I let go of his arm, which he lowered, and held his wrist as I*

sat down again in my chair.) He is walking with
me now.

Medhurst:	Where ?
George:	Here.
Medhurst:	In the studio here ?
George:	Your studio does not exist.
Medhurst:	It's just a thing we imagine, is it ?
Brian:	Are we shadows ?
George:	You are young. To me the grass is not wet. To this man it is – he steps in a puddle. (*At this point George began slowly to raise his right leg at full length, stiffly. The group watched it with interest but remained puzzled*.)
George:	He has stepped into the puddle. You wish to have proof ?
Medhurst:	(*Still puzzled*) Yes.
George:	The effect will last.
Medhurst:	What effect ? . . Is his foot wet ? (*In order to keep my hold of George I tucked his right arm under my left armpit and with both hands examined the foot he was holding in the air. I pushed the fingers of one hand down the inside of his suede leather shoe and felt a distict wetness. Surprised, I said :*) His foot *is* wet ; his foot is wet! Can I take the shoe off ? (*I pulled his right shoe off and handed it around :*)
Ann:	Soaking!
Brian:	Feel it.

I then took his sock off and there was enough water in it for me
to be able to wring it out so that the drippings trickled on to the
floor and marked the floor covering. Rita was looking at his
bare foot and she said, 'Look. Mud on his foot' and indeed, as
the photograph shows, there were stains on his otherwise clean
skin.

Once again, when he came round, I accused George of

trickery, suggesting that he had dipped his foot in the wash-basin before the sitting had begun. This was silly really, because we had had him in our grasp for more than two hours under hot film lights and any such fakery would have been pointless, for the foot would have dried off. There is no doubt that once more George had produced, psychosomatically, phenomena equivalent to stigmata. When we asked an eminent psychiatrist to comment on this effect he explained it as 'intense localised sweating.'

Needless to say George remembered nothing and utterly denied any hoaxing. We were so interested in this new manifestation of a Control that we broke a rule we normally followed of not telling him what had taken place. We said he had communicated in the voice of someone called 'Alfreda.'

As soon as the name was spoken he shot rigid, his eyes closed and he fell out of his chair on to the floor in a trance!

It was a name which, for him, worked like a hypnotist's trigger. After we had sat him up and brought him round we sipped our farewell coffee and were careful not to mention the name Alfreda again.

The 'Alfreda' sitting was one of the last we attended. By this time we reckoned we had more than enough material for a film and, for reasons I have already hinted at, the regular meetings came to an end. George had always been nervous about going on and sometimes he would say to Saunders and me, 'It's all right for you. You're making a film, but when you've got all you want you'll drop me like a hot potato and I'll be left with what? God knows!' We assured him we would not 'drop' him, nor did we do so. As I have said, George continued (and still does) to do work for us and we see him regularly. In my own opinion, the meetings had a therapeutic value for George and either because of this or in the natural order of things the phenomena at the hall subsided.

We did complete one film and it was shown in black and white on BBC 2. Our masters in the BBC were nervous about letting the film stand alone on its own base and insisted on its being shown in the framework of a studio discussion with a sceptic, Professor Eysenck, to see justice done for the cause of commonsense. Few people saw the film, for at that time BBC 2 had a very small audience ; but the TV critics saw it. R. W. Cooper writing in the *Times* Monday 8 May 1967 said :

Whatever we think about ghosts few can have remained unimpressed last night by BBC 2's *Two Steps in the Dark,* which found no conclusive answer to Brian Branston's filmed account of some strange happenings in a photographer's studio in London . . . Professor Eysenck, taking the sceptical view, said it could never be ruled out that the photographer had been told or had read of them at some time, and that his subconscious knowledge would come out under hypnosis. As for the earlier manifestations, a group of people in a high state of emotion believed that the hall was haunted, and everything would be seen and interpreted in these terms.

Writing in the *Sunday Times* 14 May 1967, Maurice Wiggin said :

Personally, I don't doubt for a moment the integrity of Brian Branston the producer, or Bob Saunders the director. Professor Eysenck's scepticism is of the bracing and indeed all-embracing sort – salutary as a cold bath – but what he was saying, really is that *nobody* can be trusted. Of course, ESP or PSI, or whatever you may choose to call it, is riddled, historically, with deception and self-deception ; but what is not ? The fact that there are charlatans in every field, as there are weeds, does not mean that no honest plant grows . . . This little series was the nearest, I think, that television has ever come to investigating psychical phenomena at all seriously. True, it proved nothing – except that there is something to be proved, or disproved.

Had we really proved nothing ? The tragic story of the real airman Charles Koopman *could* have been assimilated by George and stacked away in his unconscious. We have to remember that Koopman's home was in Hanwell and so was

George's. At the time of Mrs Brewer's murder George was eleven years old, and though I think it highly unlikely that he would have read the current newspaper accounts which I quoted earlier, it is more than likely that he heard his elders gossiping about the local killing. Still, we have to remember that it was not George who began the connection of a husband and a murdered wife and two-year-old daughter with Buckell Hall: *that* arose through an SPR investigation and an outside medium who came from the west country. In this story we have also to take into account the secret-list aircraft, the P 92/2. Once again, a supposed actor in the story, Biggs, lived in Hanwell. I think it most improbable that George could have gained any knowledge of the P 92/2 during its development days when it was a project on the secret list. He could hardly have derived any knowledge of the plane from the real Mr Biggs who claimed never to have been associated with it and to have left the Heston Aircraft Co. before the P 92/2 project started. The simplest explanation of normal access to information about the aircraft would be to say he read it in the *Flight* articles of 13 June 1946 and/or 8 July 1955. But neither of these articles indicated any 'jamming' or 'hydraulic failure' or 'failure in the rear.' There is scope here for much more research than ever I have had or shall have time for. But I wonder whether the fact that George simply lived in the vicinity of Koopman, Biggs and the P 92/2 development at Heston may not be the real key to the solution: plus, of course, the fact that George rented a hall adjacent to the murder place of Gladys Brewer and in which the murdered baby's pram had been stored.

I admit that in the murder story and the P 92/2 story we have 'proved' nothing, just as the critics said. But otherwise have we proved anything ?

Let me mention some of the odd happenings and by looking at them all together see whether or not some pattern emerges : in Buckell Hall lights go on and off without a switch being worked ; doors become unlocked though no hand turns a key ; George sees an oilcan sail across the studio ; lamps swing with no apparent cause ; George is 'held down' in the dark room, Rita is 'attacked' in the studio, a medium is pinned by a table ; a microphone records stroking and other noises and flies through the air from a table to the floor six feet away ; outsiders as well as studio workers watch 'rain' in a restricted area *inside* the studio ; week after week, the table raps out apparently interconnected messages ; an outsider writes an automatic message 'I was not guilty'; two inexplicable photographs are taken in the dark ; the camera taking the photographs is turned 180 degrees backwards on its tripod ; an egg jumps out of its box ; the photographer goes unwillingly into a trance, a 'pencil of cigarette smoke' stands upright out of his left eye and then disappears ; in his trance he sings a baby song ; film is taken during the photographer's trance states in which he produces stigmata, apparently the direct result of activities he has been concerned with during trance.

All these happenings seem to require the presence of George in order to take place ; and all of them happen in Buckell Hall.

Many of the phenomena, if indeed not all, are paralleled in accounts of poltergeists from the earliest reports. I am quite convinced that George was a poltergeist focus. People who experienced the phenomena had to be in the presence of George for anything to take place: Rita was 'attacked', Paul Bonner wrote automatically, a medium was pinned to a bench *while George was there.*

But is there something else ? Did the hall have *its* part to play in triggering off the manifestations ? From enquiries I have made I find no unusual events occurring outside and away from the hall to Rita or Paul Bonner or the two ladies who saw 'rain.' In George's case, the poltergeist activity also appears to be almost entirely confined to Buckell Hall. He discovered the parachute harness stigmata at his home, but judging from the other stigmata phenomena it seems likely that the 'harness' was on his body before he left the hall. I can find only one reported poltergeist phenomenon connected with George which did not occur at the hall ; that was a flashing on and off of Christmas tree lights at his home when no flashing device had been installed ; both his father and mother saw this happen and were puzzled by it – George apparently sensed a connection with himself and played the incident down to them. Apart from the various phenomena in the hall that we all witnessed, I myself had the 'force field' experience ; all this leads me to suppose that there was, and probably still is, something odd about Buckell Hall – it is what people commonly call 'haunted.'

I am the more led to believe in the possibility of a place being haunted by our experiences with the Ardara Avenue Spook when we were living in Ireland and by the incidents at Northfleet. Though the noises and bed-rockings there are typical of traditional poltergeist phenomena, we have to remember that the phenomena were experienced by at least four different sets of people at different times – the Maxteds, the Essex's, Mrs Harrison and the previous occupants of her house before Mrs Harrison. Mrs Harrison and the neighbour who attacked Eric Essex did in fact hear noises when the house was temporarily empty. Mrs Maxted and Mr Essex both reported seeing apparitions. One is inevitably led to suspect that the case of the Northfleet haunting was not a poltergeist manifestation at all, but a haunting without a poltergeist focus.

In such cases (if they do exist) the teasing question is who is the haunter ? Who or what could have haunted Buckell Hall ? The spirit of a murdered baby whose attachment to the place drew her mother's ghost and, apparently, her father's? This does not fit the reported case of Aircraftman Koopman and Mrs Gladys Brewer, because although both were dead at the time (Mrs Brewer murdered and Koopman hanged) Gladys Brewer's husband survived her. There is, of course, one circumstance which, if it were true, would give some credence to the hauntings and that is if Koopman should have been the father of Mrs Brewer's child! The solicitor who prepared Koopman's defence, Mr Lawrence Dennis, told our researcher that 'there was no motive for the murder.' Yet Koopman had known Mrs Brewer for five years before the murder and he had written to her husband that 'your wife is very immoral.' How did Koopman know this ? How – unless he himself was part of what he believed to be 'immoral' ? Have we here a motive for murder, a crime of passion resulting from the most powerful spurs to human action – deprivation, jealousy and sex ?

This again, we have by no means proved, but have we 'proved' anything else ? One thing I am certain of is that we all saw demonstrated the power of what for want of a better word we must call at the moment mind over matter. This power seemed to be capable of manifesting itself in at least three different ways. Certain individuals, to whom public attention is drawn when they become poltergeist foci, have the power to make objects move without touching them. This is the first manifestation of the 'power' and it is demonstrated by George's flying oilcan. Such movements appear to be at random. The second manifestation is movements of objects to which no physical force known to man is applied such as the microphone which left the table and crashed to the floor behind Saunders, the egg which jumped out of its box, and some movements of the seance table: these phenomena are not at random but appear to be caused for a purpose ; and the third manifestation of mind over matter is shown in the stigmata effects of the parachute harness, the scratch marks, the neck rope mark and the wet foot.

In George's case, I do not believe that he was conscious of producing any of these phenomena: they were the product of his unconscious mind while in a waking though disassociated state so that he had no conscious recollection of how or why or even if he himself was producing the effects. But that he could subconsciously produce the effects *at will* I believe is demonstrated by such phenomena as the wet foot.

The power to produce such phenomena – the inexplicable movement of objects at a distance and *at will,* but to do it while fully conscious and not in a trance state is demonstrated by the subject of my next chapter.

6
The Wizard of Utrecht

I don't know who first called Gerard Croiset the 'Wizard' – But the name fits.

One of my most vivid memories of this internationally celebrated Dutch clairvoyant and healer comes from a contrasty clip of 16 millimetre ciné film. It was taken as raw stock from the Germans by the Dutch Resistance during the war-time occupation of Holland, and then exposed secretly as a demonstration of Croiset's strange powers. In that film, shot thirty years ago, Croiset stands shock-haired wearing a baggy lounge suit, feet apart, arms at full stretch, fingers splayed and vibrating, exactly like a wizard of fairy tale casting a spell.

I know that I saw the astonishing event only on film. I know from my own experience that you can fake most things on film: I myself have faked anything from earthquakes to a galloping eight-legged horse. Nevertheless, I am prepared to believe that Croiset really was producing the effect that my eyes told me he was.

It was a demonstration of the power of 'mind' over matter. Gerard Croiset was forcing inanimate objects to move without actually touching them. Not only was he forcing them to move, but other people who were exerting their strength were powerless to *prevent* the objects from moving. At the time everybody, including Croiset himself, seemed to regard it as some sort of parlour trick. When I viewed the film with Croiset and his son Henri nearly thirty years later he was diffident at first about

150

showing it and – how can I express it ? – I thought I detected a feeling that he had been prostituting a power, a gift, which providence had bestowed upon him for much more serious purposes.

Let me describe part of what the film showed. Croiset was standing in a courtyard, open to the sky and surrounded on at least three sides by two-storied buildings with a gallery and open walk running around the upper floor. The yard was probably totally enclosed, but since the cameraman was standing facing Croiset and shooting forward to the end wing, one didn't see what was behind the camera. Croiset was facing the camera but his concentration and wizard-like passes were directed upwards at the end balcony behind him. Here were seated three men facing down into the well of the courtyard. They were holding in their hands T-shaped rods fashioned from thin bars of metal rather resembling the hazel twig used by a water-diviner. I suppose the stem of the T was about a foot long, while the handles protruded an inch or so outside the men's clenched fists.

They were trying to prevent the rods from turning round and round between their arms. All the rods were turning the same way and all were in time with each other.

About twenty feet below, Gerard Croiset was making his magician's passes and apparently driving the rods round and round at a steady rate of perhaps one revolution every two seconds. The effort required of Croiset made his whole body and arms vibrate as though he was being galvanized by a series of electric shocks.

A second shot showed another man gripping the extensions of a twirling T rod with all his might (judging by the expression on his face) and to help him arrest the movement, two other men were holding the rod ends protruding from the outside of the man's fists. It was all to no avail. The T-shaped rod continued steadily to turn as long as Croiset magicked it with his outstretched arms.

There were a number of bystanders on the balcony, both men and women, and judging from their broad smiles they were highly tickled at the show. They appeared to be, in a sense, independent witnesses to a happening which they regarded as a rum go, but which nevertheless *was* happening no matter how it might have been produced.

When I saw the film with Croiset he made no comment. I don't think he would have shown it to me had his son Henri not wanted it to be shown – and since Henri was working the projector there was nothing to be done. Neither of them offered any explanation: it was just something that *happened,* and you either accepted it or not as you pleased.

As for myself, I do not propose to explore the ins and outs of this strange phenomenon until my reader has made the further acquaintance of Mynheer Gerard Croiset, the Wizard of Utrecht.

Gerard Croiset is a Dutch Jew, but not an orthodox one. He is now over sixty years old. His parents were Jews but not practising ones. Apparently atheistic, the father and mother made no attempt to influence the boy one way or the other as far as religion was concerned. He attended no church but appears to be a religious man. As a child he is said to have prayed often, much to the disgust of his parents. Although he is a member of no religious sect he does appear to recognize Christ, and he himself believes that his creator has blessed him with a remarkable gift. The gift takes two forms, first what from time out of mind has been called 'second sight', and then a capacity to heal through the laying on of hands. Sceptical people will pour scorn on Croiset's activities as a healer. I have attended Croiset's 'surgery' at his home and the forty or fifty patients waiting for treatment were in no way sceptical. Croiset's home used to be at Enschede in eastern Holland, and at the time I met him, he was holding a regular weekly surgery there as well as in Utrecht. Dutch people came to consult him about their ailments from all over Holland. At my first 'surgery' I met a working man who was travelling once a week from Eindhoven for treatment of a bowel complaint which his doctors had told him was incurable. But, he claimed, Croiset *was* curing him. I asked him particularly if he needed to have faith. 'Not at all', he replied, 'Mr Croiset is a healer and he does the work'. I might mention here that another war-time clip of film shown to me had Croiset apparently healing a dog paralysed in its legs. It had been run over and the resulting spinal injury had paralysed its hind quarters. The dog's owner, a woman, had the animal on her knee. Croiset made passes over the animal's back after which it came down from its owner's lap and walked. It would be silly to claim that the dog showed faith or was influenced psychologically – whatever else one might think.

At the second surgery I attended, three men came in who were obviously not locals. Their speech was double dutch even to the Dutchmen. Two of them were from the far north of Norway and the third was an interpreter. One of the two from Norway had been brought all the way from beyond the Arctic circle by his father to get treatment from Croiset. After the first couple of sessions they were to return home and Croiset would continue the treatment by remote control.

I watched Croiset's methods keenly. When the surgery was lined with patients sitting on chairs all round the walls of the long ground floor room of his house, Croiset would make his entrance. He struck me as being well aware of the value of a little showmanship. A rustle of expectancy from the patients. Croiset went and stood by an empty chair in the middle of the room and called the first sufferer to sit down. The whole atmosphere was informal, even light-hearted, with Croiset cracking the occasional joke and the other patients joining in the laughter. Since the exchanges were in Dutch, I had no chance of finding out whether new patients indicated their symptoms or whether Croiset began his treatment at once without asking for any information. At any rate, the healer would quickly start work on the head, eyes, ears, back or legs of the individual. He placed one of his hands somewhere on the patient's body, keeping it in contact. This was usually his left hand. His right hand made passes over the affected part without actually touching it. After a time, say two or three minutes,

F

when the treatment was nearing an end, he would jerk the passing hand away as if he were casting out the offending symptoms.

After treating a number of patients (including children in arms) he would sit down, tired, as though power had gone from him. I saw a grey-haired woman of fifty or more being wheeled into his consulting room by her friends. She was paralysed. Her wheelchair was pushed to the middle of the room, and when her turn came, Croiset put his left hand on her shoulder and began to make passes two or three inches above her left wrist which lay useless along the arm rest of her invalid chair. What I saw next struck me very forcibly. The paralysed arm began to jerk as though some sort of magnetism was affecting it from the passes being made over it by Croiset's hand. I have no explanation to offer for this phenomenon. I can only say that the woman's arm moved when Croiset was making his passes and stopped when he stopped. I am strongly given to believe that the same sort of power was coming from Croiset and affecting the woman's arm as I had seen in the film clip when the iron bars turned.

Most people are extremely sceptical of claims made by healers. Professional scientists, doctors, psychologists and psychiatrists frankly regard healers as quacks imposing on a gullible public. If cures seem to be obtained, then the professionals explain them away as being brought about by auto-suggestion, by the patient's own subconscious mind affecting his physical condition. Or, as in the case of the dog, by nature simply taking a turn for the better. However, from enquiring I discovered that some physicians were recommending their hopeless patients (like the man from Eindhoven) to seek Croiset's help. But whether this was because the physicians believed their patients *were* beyond hope and that Croiset could neither kill nor cure, I was never able to find out.

The healing side of Croiset's activities must, as far as I am concerned, remain a puzzle. Some doctors attribute Croiset's successes to 'vital force', bodily changes of metabolism, stimulation of blood or glands, or just natural recovery. Long and careful experimental study would be necessary before one could draw any worthwhile conclusions, and so far, few qualified persons have been eager to – shall I say ? – waste their time. In 1949 a psychiatrist attached to the University of Amsterdam hospital studied groups of patients who claimed to have been 'healed' by Croiset. He concluded that Croiset used 'suggestion' to make seemingly paralysed muscles work, and to bring an increased blood supply to the body. With the other side of Croiset's gift, his 'second sight', the situation is entirely different: for he has long been the centre of intensive study made by Doctor W. H. C. Tenhaeff, Professor of parapsychology at Utrecht University.

In 1956 Gerard Croiset, who was then living in the textile town of Enschede near the German border, moved to the ancient university town of Utrecht in order to be near Professor Willem Tenhaeff to facilitate the professor's study of Croiset's 'second sight'. I have so far used this popular traditional term 'second sight' because it is commonly understood. Once the professors move in, the term is seen to be vague and lacking in standing so attempts are made to gain both precision and class by coining more pedantic names. Second sight has usually been understood to mean the ability to see what is going to happen in the future. But the people who claim to have this power frequently assert that they are able to see what is happening out of their normal eyesight in the present, as well as what has happened in the past. A common term for possessors of the gift is 'clairvoyant'. Professor Tenhaeff has coined another name, 'paragnost', from two Greek words *para* meaning 'beyond' and *gnosis* meaning 'knowledge'. Such names give an air of respectability to a subject which most people still regard as raffish and definitely 'beyond belief'. Nobody could be more respectable and donnish than Professor Tenhaeff, a traditional university type in a university which goes back some three and a half centuries as a seat of learning. But Tenhaeff moves with the times and has for years made use of the tape-recorder in his study of Croiset. Croiset now has a tape-recorder plugged into his telephone and records conversations for the benefit of Tenhaeff. Because I needed respectability for my BBC film it was through Professor Tenhaeff that I made my approach to Gerard Croiset.

Having produced two films on what is commonly believed to be the 'supernatural' for television, I was anxious to make a third with a subject who for years had literally been taped by a professional scientist. I will say at once that Professor Tenhaeff was dubious about Croiset's 'healing' activities. Tenhaeff himself has steered clear of them and he gave me the impression that he wouldn't like to see them figure in any film we should do. Tenhaeff's assistant at the Utrecht University Institute of Parapsychology, Miss Nicky Louwerens, was even more set against the healing (it seemed to me) than her boss. Nevertheless, I made it plain that I felt we must present a rounded picture of Croiset in the film and therefore some account of his healing activities would have to be included. Perhaps I ought to have taken more notice of their demurring, for in the end it was just these healing sequences which gave my own bosses in the BBC cold feet, and our Croiset film was never shown on BBC television.

However, let me indicate the credentials and attitude of the man I was asking to be my sponsor with Gerard Croiset.

As a young man, Tenhaeff became interested in training to be a psychologist. Early on, he found himself drawn to what he himself calls the 'frontier science of psychology' namely parapsychology, which deals with 'paranormal phenomena'. In 1933 the University of Utrecht gave Tenhaeff the chance to teach parapsychology there as a *privaat docent* or unpaid external lecturer. At that time he had already done research work in the parapsychology field and had written some books. Progress was slow, but not to be sneered at, for how many universities in the world even today have full time parapsychology lecturers? After nearly twenty years, the University of Utrecht made an honest man of Tenhaeff when in 1951 he was taken into the fold as a lecturer on the staff. Two years later, in 1953, Doctor Tenhaeff was appointed professor of Parapsychology *extra-ordinarius* – a term which somehow suggests a post which still has not entirely established its respectability. At the same time, he was made Director of the University's Institute of Parapsychology.

Professor Tenhaeff has worked in the field of extra-sensory perception for over fifty years and continually tested the men and women he has dubbed *paragnosts* – 'a man or woman you can use for experiments in extra-sensory perception or *paragnosy*'. His most celebrated guinea-pig is no doubt Gerard Croiset.

As early as 1920, the doyen of Dutch academical psychology and founder of the Dutch Society for Psychical Research, Professor Heymans, indicated the need to carry out extensive personality research on people known as telepathists and clairvoyants. About 1926, Tenhaeff began collecting as much data as possible from biographies and autobiographies of paragnosts as well as contacting living people in order to form, as he says, a picture of their personality structure. He found that some paragnosts disliked investigation while others were interested in having their gifts scientifically researched and willing to serve as subjects. Of the fifty or so tested by Tenhaeff, Gerard Croiset is, he says, 'one of those paragnosts who see the great utility of scientific research of his gifts and this is one of many reasons why he is a very good subject'.

Between 1954 and 1957 Tenhaeff tested at his institute forty-seven people reported to be paragnosts. His findings are worth thinking about. He says 'in the case of the male paragnosts their masculinity is hidden under a feminine surface and in the case of the female paragnosts their femininity is hidden under a masculine surface. Also, disintegration of the personality is one of the characteristics of paragnosts examined by us. Our research pointed out that, generally speaking, the paragnost stands closer to primitive man and the child than the strongly individualised cultured man. Several of the subjects observed and examined by us did not show that individual unity of thinking, feeling and willing peculiar to well-integrated or harmonious people.[1] According to Tenhaeff many paragnosts

[1]Transcript of a filmed interview at Utrecht 25 May 1967.

perform 'in states in which the level of consciousness is lowered. In this state there is a tendency to think in visual terms'. He goes on to say,

We are not only interested in what our subjects see. We also want to know in what way they see it. I will give you an example out of hundreds. During a sitting one of our subjects asked a Swedish lady who was fully unknown to him what that apple meant that he saw with her: 'I see an apple with you. It must have something to do with Paradise. It is a representation of the beginning of the world. You have something to do with Paradise. *Would your name be Eve ?'* The lady answered that her name was Eve. Then he got in a similar way an impression of the name of the street where the lady was living in Stockholm and the number of her house. On another occasion, during a test the clairvoyant said to a man, 'You live at an odd numbered house. Could it be 101 ?' The man in question answered that he lived in number 101. When we asked the subject how he came to get 101, he said that the chimneypiece in the house of his parents had appeared to him. On the chimneypiece stood a statuette of the Holy Family with the infant Jesus, placed under a round glass bell. This round bell (which reminded him of a nought) was flanked by two high glass bells which reminded him of the figure one. When we compare these examples with hundreds of others, we find a remarkable comformity. There is a curious cropping up of associated pictures. These associates can easily cause errors by wrong interpretation. We have large collections of these wrong interpretations.[1]

Doctor Tenhaeff gives an example of associated imagery from the dreams of Professor Kooy, an internationally known expert in space travel. Tenhaeff met Professor Kooy for the first time in 1932 and began studying Kooy's dreams. For three years, on waking every morning, Kooy faithfully recorded his memories of his dreams. He made two copies of the record, sending one to Tenhaeff for examination. Investigation revealed

[1]As above.

that not only the recent past but also the near future was reflected in Kooy's dreams. Statistical tests convinced Tenhaeff that the dreams foretelling the future could not have occurred by chance. An appreciable portion of the dream material which Doctor Kooy provided proved to be connected with unexpected deaths. About a year before Kooy began his tests with Tenhaeff he had lost his father to whom he had been greatly attached. Professor Tenhaeff was convinced that Professor Kooy's dream images displayed a strong associative relation to the loss he had suffered. Tenhaeff says:

In my opinion parapsychologists, when collecting spontaneous cases, should trace their deep psychological background . . . The man in the street has the wrong opinion that a paragnost is able to see everything he wishes to. This is not the case. All these subjects have their specialisations, and these specialisations have often to do with experiences they have had in their youth . . . That Croiset had many good results with missing and drowned children has to do with a shocking experience he had when he was 8 years old. In my opinion Croiset would not have had these results but for that experience.[1]

Professor Tenhaeff is of the opinion that the paragnosy or extra-sensory perception – ESP as it has come to be called – is a natural phenomenon. He says 'It is latent in all of us. It has been lost with civilisation. When I say it has been lost with civilisation this is not to say that there is no possibility that it won't come back. I believe it will come back'.

It has been said that the work of Doctor Tenhaeff, the Director of the Parapsychology Institute at the University of Utrecht, is possibly a generation ahead of the more limited psychical researches in Great Britain and that he probably knows more about paranormal phenomena than any other scholar alive. This then was the man who agreed to introduce me to Gerard Croiset, without doubt his star subject.

[1] As above.

The idea of making a film about Gerard Croiset first came to me after I had read a book called *Croiset the Clairvoyant* written by an American, Jack Harrison Pollack, and published by the Quality Book Club in Britain in 1965. What swayed me to go forward into what most reasonable people regard as a twilight area of phoney spiritualist mediums, clairvoyants, fortune-tellers and their dupes was the testimony and standing of Professor Tenhaeff, which are well brought out in Pollack's book. I regard myself as being sceptical but intensely curious about odd phenomena. I am also a cautious man. Even though the written evidence was overwhelmingly in Croiset's favour, I had to think of the BBC's reputation – as well as my own – and so I journeyed to Holland to interview the protagonists. I wanted to size everything up for myself. My first interviews in Utrecht were with Professor Tenhaeff and his hard-headed assistant Miss Louwerens. As I have written, these two were against much publicising of Croiset's healing activities ; nevertheless, they were happy to introduce me to their star subject and to help set up any filming of his ESP gifts. Late in the afternoon Mr Croiset came to the Professor's rooms where I was introduced to him and eventually driven by him to his home at 21 Willem de Zwijgerstraat. There I met his wife and one of his sons, Henri, who acts as his father's interpreter. I was shown the film clips I have already described, and I attended a healing session. At the end of two days I was convinced that Croiset was as genuine as Professor Tenhaeff had believed him to be and that we had excellent material for a film documentary. We would cover a number of missing persons cases already solved by Croiset ; the filmed episodes of the injured dog and the twisting metal rod ; his healing ; and we would stage a fairly elaborate 'chair test' which would demonstrate Croiset's powers of extra-sensory perception in a controlled experiment. In addition, largely to satisfy my own doubts, I was determined to throw in a test about which neither Croiset nor Doctor Tenhaeff nor anybody else but myself would have any prior knowledge. I knew that such a test might be regarded by Croiset as a trick and therefore give him offence and even ruin

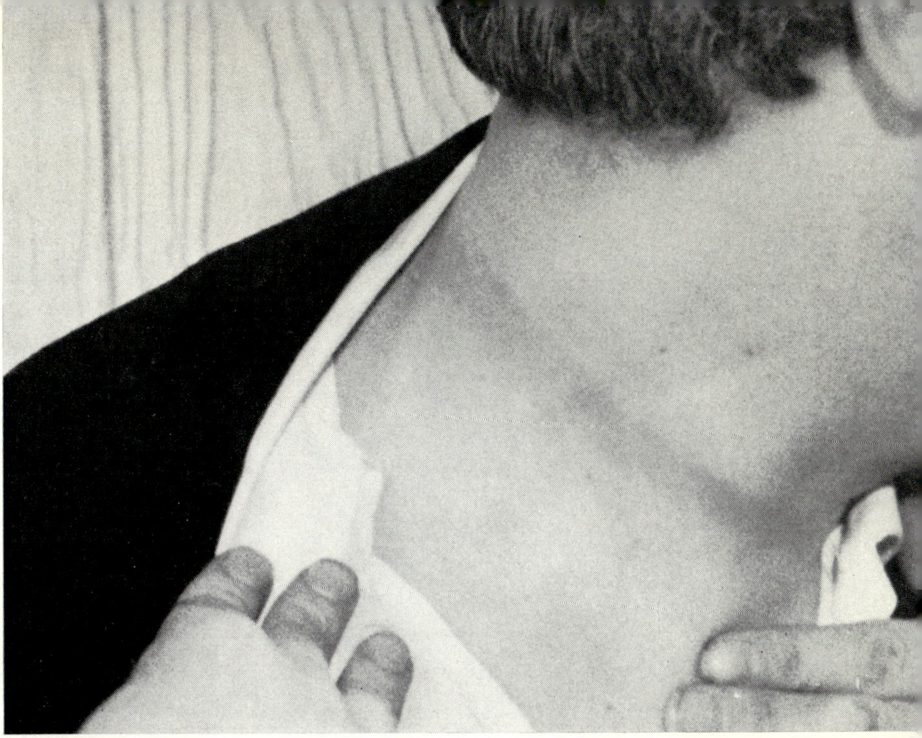

Above Stigmata: the rope mark on George's neck. 'How far round does it go?'

Below George's muddy foot and soaking sock

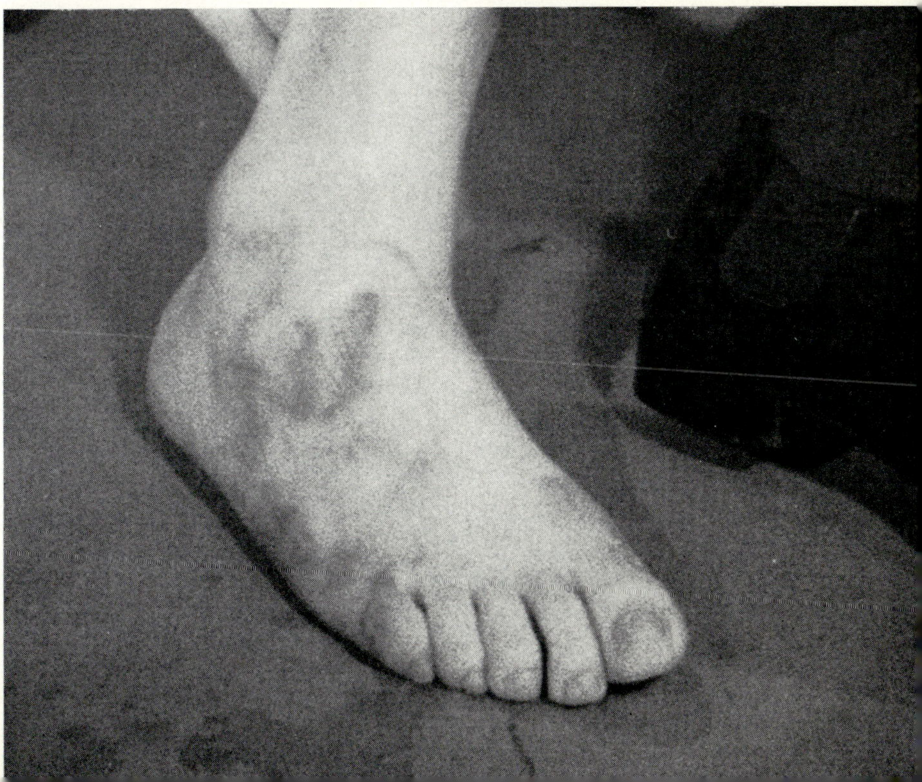

Left
Croiset – the wizard of Utrecht

Below
They were holding in their hands T-shaped rods

Opposite
Croiset treating a child

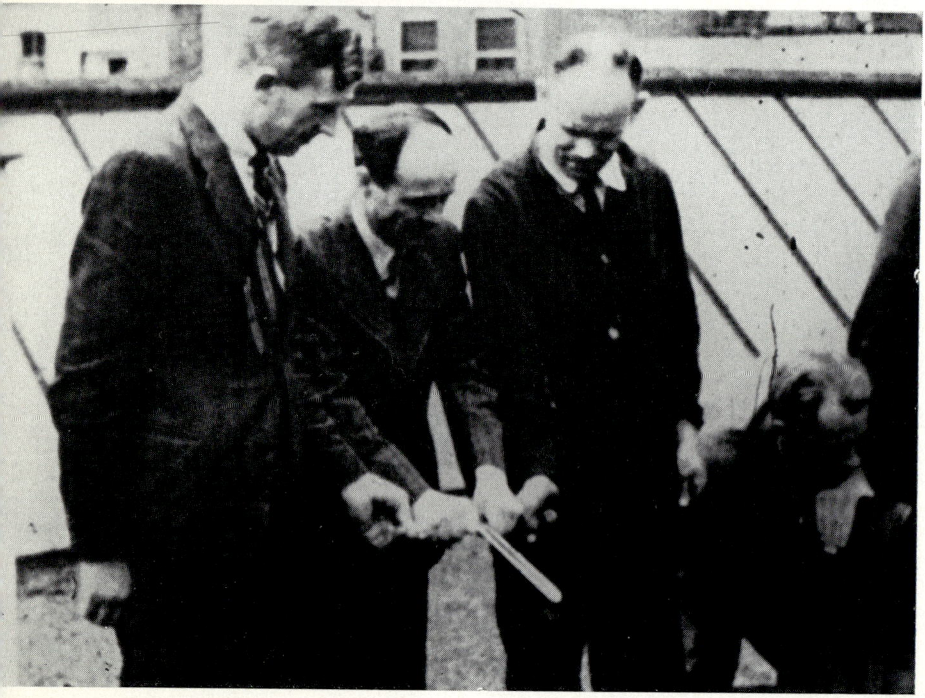

Left

The chair test – 'a hole in the material covering the right leg'

Below

'Has there been an attack on a Kibbutz?' The newspaper reads 'Attack on Kibbutz'.

the whole project; nevertheless, for my own satisfaction I reckoned the risk worth taking. If Croiset proved himself in *my* test, then I would be that much more convinced of the genuineness of his powers.

Back at the BBC I discussed plans with my colleague Bob Saunders who had played so large a part in the Buckell Hall and Poltergeist films. I asked him to take over the setting up of the Croiset film which he would direct and which I would produce. We arranged to collaborate with Dutch Television and to use a Dutch film crew. The time agreed on for the filming, which would be in two parts, was April and May 1967. There had to be two separate filmings in order to meet the requirements of the Chair Test: the first would show Croiset making a series of prophecies about a person who would sit in a certain chair at a meeting to be called six weeks after the prophecy; the second lot of filming would cover the main sequences in the documentary plus the meeting at which an unknown person would occupy a chair unknown at the time of the prophecy. This chair test, which I shall describe in detail later, was first devised for Croiset by Tenhaeff in 1947. Since then it has been successfully carried out over 400 times in Holland, Germany, Austria, Italy and Switzerland. If the acceptance of an experiment by scientists depends on its being capable of being repeated, then Croiset's Chair Test must surely have proved itself. What happened with our Chair Test we shall see.

We began our film, then, with a reference to the fact that Gerard Croiset has been called on by the police of the Netherlands and half a dozen other countries including the USA and Russia to help find missing persons and to solve baffling crimes. Croiset is frequently rung up on the telephone for help and this is perhaps the way in which he prefers to be approached. He feels that a telephone call helps to eliminate outside influences and to reduce overlapping impressions which can, and have been known to, set him off on a wrong track.

In April 1963 a little boy of eight, Kesh Mollart, disappeared

161

from his house in the Hague. He was a friendly little chap who had set out for school but never arrived. Each morning on his way he passed, first, his grandmother's house and then a fish and chip shop kept by an uncle and aunt. When the boy did not return home his father notified the police. A night passed and there was no news. The agitated father decided to phone Gerard Croiset. The paragnost did in fact give the father certain information which proved to be of no help. Another day passed and the boy's father went to Croiset's home in Utrecht and begged Croiset for some real assistance. Croiset thereupon made a number of statements and drew a sketch. The sketch included a wooden sandbox (painted blue, said Croiset) with an iron bar and an iron lock on it, a boat, a bridge and a clock tower. The clairvoyant also described a large building with a lot of glittering silver windows. All this information could have been of no help to the distracted parents for the little boy was already drowned. But at this time nobody (except perhaps Croiset) knew this.

When the father, Mynheer Mollart, got back to the Hague he was contacted by a journalist, Henk Huigen, who covered the story in his paper, described the landmarks postulated by Croiset and published Croiset's drawing.

Four days after the newspaper had been published, little Kesh Mollart's body was found in the harbour. There was no suggestion of foul play. He had obviously fallen into the water and drowned. His body was discovered within the landmarks described by Croiset – the blue wooden sandbox with the iron bar and lock ; a boat which was in fact tethered for use as a floating office, a sort of permanent fixture ; a bridge and a clock tower. There was also a large factory building with many windows. Croiset had said *silvery* windows and the journalist Henk Huigen's theory of this was as follows: 'Croiset told he saw a building with glittering silvery windows and that's possible, for the last view of the boy was at a time that the sun was going down over there and then when you are there with your head on the water in the middle of the harbour the sun is coming in that window and they will be glittering. They will be silvery'.

Tenhaeff's verbatim observation was this: 'Well, very important is the fact that Mr Huigen, who was present when there was a consultation of Croiset by the parents of the child, he put what Croiset said in the newspaper, the drawing Croiset made before the corpse of the child was found, everyone who read the newspapers could control it. So thousands of men and women were in a position to control the rightness of what Croiset had said'.

The points of interest in this case (it seems to me) are that Croiset achieves contact with an extraordinary happening, an accident possibly involving death, through the intermediary of close relatives. He then in a flash sees pictures of the *surroundings* in which the accident has happened or where a discovery of a body will be made. Henk Huigen's explanation of the silvery windows may hold a clue as to *how* the clairvoyant obtains some of his information. The factory windows were only silvery on occasions when the sun happened to be in a certain position and the observer in another position. If the drowning boy saw this silvery phenomenon, then apparently Croiset was experiencing it through the intermediary of the boy's mind – but at a time when the boy was already 'dead'.

A second example of Croiset's intervention in a missing child case brings up further points of interest which I will mention after describing the incident. A four-year-old boy, Japie de Klerk, went missing from his home in Haarlem near the Dutch North Sea Coast at a time when Croiset was living in Enschede, the full breadth of Holland away – about 100 miles as the crow flies. One evening in April 1954, Haarlem Police Inspector Willem Gorter was visited in his home by the family of the little boy, Japie, and asked by them to telephone Croiset for his help. Inspector Gorter complied with their wishes and, having got through by long-distance to Croiset, was surprised to hear the clairvoyant say, 'Tell me nothing. I know that you will tell me that in Haarlem is a child that is missing and I will tell you something about the child'. Inspector Gorter says that Croiset 'told me that this child was four or five or six years old . . . He was not sure of the age. He was lying in a river near a bridge . . . Near the bridge he saw a caravan and four or five trucks and bales of peat, a shipyard and a derrick near the bridge. He said he was clear that the child was dead'.[1] Croiset also told Inspector Gorter that he would find the drowned boy after three or four days.

From the description given by Croiset, the Inspector decided that the bridge referred to must be over the river Spirna near the de Klerks' home. He found such a bridge as fitted with the other information given by the clairvoyant and sure enough, after three or four days, the little boy's drowned body was discovered in the water.

The similarities in these two cases are the instigation of an approach by the parents of the missing child to Croiset, the apparent perception at a great distance by Croiset of a landscape: it is as if the paragnost had in his possession the All-Seeing Eye of Arabian fairy tale ; and the landscape is one with figures – the figures of the dead children. In both cases Croiset appeared to be aware that the children were already dead – he had perception of an event which had already taken place but not brought to his cognisance by normal sensory channels. In the case of Japie de Klerk there was something more: somehow Croiset knew what the Police Inspector was going to tell him before Gorter was given a chance to do so ; in addition he was able to see into the future and tell the Inspector when he would find the body.

In these two incidents, at least three reputable witnesses, Professor Tenhaeff, Police Inspector Gorter and the journalist Henk Huigen are convinced that Croiset demonstrated powers of seeing what had happened in the past, what was happening in the present, and what was about to happen in the future, all by extra-sensory perception. In knowing what Inspector Gorter's phone call was about there is *prima facie* evidence that Croiset was mind-reading. Such powers are difficult to credit at second-hand and for the purpose of allaying my own nagging doubts I decided (as I have said) to spring a test on Mynheer Croiset without warning. My own test would also concern a missing person and, in order to give Croiset a link with the subject, I

[1]Quotations from a filmed interview at Inspector Gorter's home at Hemstede near Haarlem on 22 May 1967.

would produce an object which he could handle and so practice psychometry, defined by the Oxford English Dictionary as 'the (alleged) faculty of divining, from physical contact or proximity only, the qualities or properties of an object, or of persons or things that have been in contact with it'. The object that I wanted Croiset to psychometrise from was a letter written by Sir John Franklin.

Sir John Franklin was a British naval officer who first entered the service at the age of fourteen. He fought under Nelson at Trafalgar and afterwards, like many naval officers during periods of comparative peace, became interested in Polar exploring. Off and on, from the year 1819 until 1827 he made extensive land journeys along the Coppermine river and the Canadian arctic coast including a descent of the Mackenzie river. He was knighted in 1829 and after a spell as governor of Van Diemen's land, now called Tasmania, he sailed from England in command of two naval vessels, the *Erebus* and *Terror,* to try to discover the presumed North West Passage between the Atlantic and Pacific Oceans. The two ships, with 129 men on board, sailed in 1845 and after passing through Lancaster Sound above Baffin Island some 250 miles from the North Pole, disappeared, as it seemed, from the face of the earth.

For the next twenty years, expedition after expedition was dispatched by government as well as private individuals to search for Franklin. Finally, his fate and that of his ships and crews was pieced together from reports by Eskimos, some of whom were found to have relics from the expedition; but it was not until 1858 that the actual message was discovered. It had been scribbled on the margin of an official form and left for preservation in a cairn. An Ulsterman, Captain McClintock, leading an expedition of twenty-four men in the steam yacht *Fox,* found the message after a perilous journey, thirteen years after the expedition began. It stated that the two ships *Erebus* and *Terror* had been beset in September 1846 and clamped into the frozen sea of Victoria Strait for two years; that Franklin

165

had died on 11 June 1847 ; and that the survivors were then on their way south over the ice in an attempt to reach the arctic coast of Canada. Even after this, further search parties continued to seek the survivors. None were ever found. Some may have stayed with Eskimos. The others, weakened with starvation and cold, probably died of scurvy in the vast desert of ice and snow.

Sir John Franklin, then, was the 'missing person' I wanted Croiset to give me information about, and to trigger him off I took with me to Holland a letter written by Franklin in 1845 shortly before leaving England on his attempt to find the North-West Passage. I had already used this letter (without success) in a previous psychometrical test of Miss Geraldine Cummins. The letter had been masked within a wide cardboard mount which hid the superscription and signature. For the Cummins test, the few visible lines of writing were left open; in the Croiset test I had the letter given to him in a sealed envelope. We had set up our camera in Croiset's home in Utrecht and the presenter of the programme, a bi-lingual Dutchman, Gerton van Wageningen, had been briefly told that we wanted to spring a test without prior notice on Croiset. Croiset himself was under the impression that van Wageningen was to do a general filmed interview and the clairvoyant's manner demonstrated distinct annoyance when he realised that he was being tested. Bob Saunders was directing the camera crew and I took from my pocket the sealed Franklin letter and handed it to him. He passed it on, still sealed, to van Wageningen and the camera was given the order to roll.

The contents of the letter were quite inconsequential and even if Croiset had been allowed a chance of reading it, he would have gained little information. Had the letter been opened and seen by Croiset to begin with, he might have got a clue from the style of writing and the faded paper. But it wasn't opened until he had made his first report. Only Saunders and I knew that the envelope contained Franklin's letter. The letter was written to an unknown clergyman and ran:

166

My dear sir,

Could you do my sister and myself the kindness of getting us seats at your church this morning. I am particularly anxious to go there with her and will you say by the bearer at which door we are to enter.

Ever yours most sincerely,

John Franklin.

I will now give a verbatim transcript of the English part of two synchronous camera 'takes' which cover the test:

Gerton van Wageningen: This envelope was given to me by Bob Saunders, the director of the programme and he asked me to ask some questions about it to Mr Croiset. I don't know anything about what's in, except that it's a letter. Here it is. Now I ask Mr Croiset to tell me something about the letter. Mynheer Croiset ... (*asks Croiset in Dutch to say what impressions he gets from the letter. Croiset holds the letter.*)

Croiset: (*speaks in Dutch with van Wageningen giving running translation into English*): I have an idea ... a document about a ... from a former century. It deals with ... Question – is this handwriting authentic ? Is my opinion correct ?

G.v.W.: (*translating what he said to Croiset*): I don't know anything about it, neither does Mr Saunders. I think it has to do with a missing person.

Croiset: (*running translation by G.v.W.*): This is long ago. This is from a former century ... from an early ... from history. (*I had been watching Croiset closely and up to this point he seemed to be floundering. Suddenly his whole facial expression changed, a light came into his eyes and I thought to myself 'By Jove! He's got on to the beam!'*) Is it a man who has been on a ship ? A sailor ? A high ranked officer. A sort of marine ... he drowned with a sort of marine ship. I see he has a job on a marine ship ... a ship is sinking and then he disappears. He disappears with the ship. Between America and England. Atlantic Ocean. 1866 or 1869. I'm sorry ... 1866 or 1868.

G.v.W.: May I open the letter ? (*He opens the letter*).

Croiset: (*G.v.W. translating*) This man has been a captain on a ship, captain of a ship ... The ship was wrecked in ... was sunk in the Atlantic Ocean. That's what I see about it.[1]

Croiset: (*G.v.W. translating*) The very first impression that I got ... that it had to do with the 16th or 17th century. Um ... and with 1866 and 1868. That's what struck me. And a man who disappeared with a ship ... with his ship ... The ship is broken in two parts in the middle. That's all. Thank you. Thanks to you.[2]

My reaction on hearing Croiset's statements was one of surprise bordering on astonishment – counting the number of hits makes it impossible (in my opinion) to deny that the clairvoyant was receiving a true extra-sensory impression of the loss of Sir John Franklin. First, we have to notice that Gerton van Wageningen was not really translating the Dutch word *marine* used by Croiset. In Dutch *marine* means 'naval' or 'navy'. So what Croiset said when tabulated was as follows:

The letter concerned:

1. *Events from 'history'*. (Correct)
2. *Events from a 'former century'* (Correct. I believe that Croiset used this phrase to draw a distinction between long-past events and the problems he was usually asked to elucidate which invariably concerned people recently missing.)
3. *Events from the 16th and 17th centuries* (Wrong)
4. *A man on a ship, a sailor.* (Correct)

[1]Slate 104, take 3.
[2]Slate 105, take 1.

5. *A high ranking officer.* (Correct. Franklin was in supreme command)

6. *A 'sort of' naval officer.* (Absolutely correct, for Franklin was commanding a naval expedition sent out by the Admiralty but not a fighting or patrolling assignment.)

7. *A captain of a ship.* (Correct. Franklin commanded the *Erebus.*)

8. *An officer who drowned.* (Wrong)

9. *A sinking ship.* (Probably correct. After being beset in the ice it is more than likely that the *Erebus* broke up and sank.)

10. *A ship broken in two parts in the middle.* (Probably correct. See 9.)

11. *A ship sunk between America and England.* (Correct.)

12. *A ship sunk in the Atlantic Ocean.* (Correct. I don't believe anyone has defined precisely at what point in the North-West Passage the Atlantic Ocean begins. In layman's terms Victoria Strait is, as far as I am concerned, still the Atlantic.)

13. *Events in the year 1866 or 1868.* (Wrong. Although Franklin died in 1847, news of his death was not made known to the outside world before 1858 when McClintock found the expedition's message: so one could say that Croiset was 10 years out – not a bad estimate in the case of an event which had taken place almost 100 years before his statement.)

If we summarise Croiset's comments on the Franklin letter, we find that out of thirteen statements he has produced eight correct, two probably correct and three wrong. Such results are quite beyond the possibility of chance. My test had served its purpose. The results were more than enough to convince me that Gerard Croiset possesses a sixth sense which is either dormant or non-existent in normal people – a sense which ought to be investigated and publicised.

Before leaving the Franklin test I want to call attention to two significant points: first, Croiset appeared to me at the beginning to be struggling to attain 'contact'; as far as I could detect by watching his facial expression 'contact' came in a flash and after that information was imparted without a struggle. The second interesting point, I believe, is that Croiset seemed to be getting his information through pictures flashed on to a mental retina. This could sometimes lead him to a faulty interpretation: for instance, he received pictures of a dead ship's captain and of a broken ship and his conclusion, therefore, was that the Captain had drowned. It was a logical assumption but a mistake, for Franklin died of what are called 'natural causes'.

Such mistakes afford in my opinion a valuable clue to this extraordinary sense possessed by certain gifted people. They are not omniscient, they do not possess a 'supernatural' power. They have a facility which enables them to perceive through time and space. But just as a normal person, usually able to apprehend only through his five senses, can make mistakes of interpretation, so can clairvoyants.

Such a test as I devised for Croiset's clairvoyancy was hardly possible in connection with his healing. We *did* take a young doctor with us to Holland to hold a watching brief, but ultimately our main function as far as the healing was concerned, was to give as unbiassed a report as possible without attempting to draw conclusions.

I will give an account of some of the patients we met and filmed in Croiset's consulting room. First, the testimony of a Mr Dokkum:

I'll tell you I've two vertebrae which are too flat. I've gone through several silent waiting rooms of doctors. And I've been operated on in hospital. It was a diagnostic operation (*one to find out the cause of the trouble*) and couldn't help me. Still, I trusted to science, but my family, my parents said, 'Go to Mr Croiset. Perhaps he can help you'. And I went to this room. I saw a man in the middle in this chair here, and after those sittings in (*ordinary doctors'*) silent waiting rooms,

I thought 'It's a theatre here!' (*referring to the laughing, joking, informal atmosphere of Croiset's 'surgery' to which I have already drawn attention*) And after an hour I wished to be away, for two reasons: for that hard chair (I was sitting on) and for the 'theatre' . . . But at that moment Mr Croiset asked me, 'Mr Dokkum! . . . I feel you can't sit longer on that hard chair!' Then I came and he put his hand on my back, just on the place and he said, 'That's the place, isn't it ?'

'Yes'.

'You haven't pain,' he said, 'it's like you have a boulder on your shoulder'. This was an amazing conclusion for me. For the doctors asked me, 'Where do you have pain ?' and I had to say, 'I haven't *pain* – it's like you have a boulder on your shoulder.' And it was Mr Croiset who knew it at once and who helped me. And I am living easier now for I am able to work hard 16 hours a day.[1]

What Mr Dokkum was testifying to became more and more apparent as our interviews went on: by some sixth sense, Croiset divined a patient's symptoms or complaint without the subject needing to give him any kind of verbal information. The effect of this on the patient was usually one of surprise leading to confidence in the clairvoyant's healing powers.

The young English doctor, Christine Pickard, whom we took with us, put it like this: 'As a doctor, I'm all too familiar with that institution, the doctor's surgery. This might look like surgery night, but it's actually the clinic of Gerard Croiset. He's not a trained doctor, of course, but he calls himself a healer – *not* a faith healer. He diagnoses by what can only be called clairvoyant methods and he treats by the laying on of hands.' This laying on of hands was simplicity itself. As I have already said, Croiset would hold his left hand on a patient's shoulder or back and then run his right hand with slow strokes over the affected part of the body – usually without making contact.

Doctor Pickard decided to experience this herself and asked Croiset to 'lay his hands' on her. She reported:

[1]Quotations taken from interviews filmed in Utrecht 24 May, 1967.

For my own part I couldn't undergo the 'treatment' because I wasn't ill. But I did try to see if Mr Croiset could evoke any sensations in me. I had been told by numerous patients and other people that when he puts his hands over you like this it causes a tingling. So I tried this, and while his hand was here, I concentrated very hard on the point underneath it, and expected to feel something there. To my great relief, I didn't. I could remain in my scepticism. But then to my surprise I found the finger tips of *both* hands begin to tingle and my fingers on the left hand moved a little and I saw and felt the muscles here twitch. This I couldn't understand at all. It could have been mere suggestion, but no-one had told me this would happen.

Doctor Pickard interviewed a man who didn't speak English through Gerton van Wageningen. His name was Stoof and he was a thatcher by trade. She reported as follows:

This man (Mynheer Stoof) seven years ago started to suffer from bad balance. He kept falling over six or seven times a day. He's a thatcher by trade which means he works high on houses putting straw on the roofs. So as you can imagine, bad balance didn't exactly help his work and he would often find himself on the ground unconscious – sometimes after falling quite a distance – without knowing quite how it happened. So of course he went to the doctor's. They diagnosed a brain tumour. They operated and found it was too extensive and they could do nothing about it. They told him it was inoperable and that he would gradually get worse. His bad balance continued and he couldn't possibly have gone back to work. He was so desperate that, although he was very sceptical, at the same time he eventually came to see Mr Croiset and started having treatment regularly. After about two weeks he started to notice an improvement. His balance started to get a little better – even though he couldn't believe it still. And after 4 weeks he was considerably improved and even fit to go back to work. That was about 4 years ago. When his specialist heard about it he was quite amazed, and said, 'Well, the only thing you can do is to keep on believing in Croiset.' Now the doctors have written him off their list altogether and he doesn't need even to go back for check-ups. His balance, he tells me, is completely normal. Before, he had to stand with his legs wide apart because other wise he just couldn't keep upright when with his eyes shut he had to hang on to walls and benches. Now, as I shall demonstrate in a moment, with eyes shut he can stay upright very well – and he is working happily again as a thatcher. (*To Mynheer Stoof*): Would you like to stand up for me? Now just stand still. You see his balance is very good. Quite normal. All right, shut your eyes (*G.v. Wageningen translates the request into Dutch*) and again it's perfectly normal. And even for a normal person it's a little difficult to stand quite still with your eyes closed. You try it.

Another case which I have already mentioned (the men from Arctic Norway) illustrates other aspects of Croiset's methods, first, treatment over long distances without laying on of hands, and second, diagnosis by clairvoyance without the patient being present.

Here is a transcript from the film 'takes' in Croiset's house on 24 May 1967:

Gerton van Wageningen: The patient in Mr Croiset's chair is Mr Arnold Fosbakk all the way from Norway, from within the Arctic circle. Mr Fosbakk, when did you fly here to Utrecht?

Fosbakk: Today.

G.v.W.: Today?

Fosbakk: But I was at Amsterdam airport yesterday.

G.v.W.: And why did you decide to come to Holland all the way from Norway?

Fosbakk: Because I have something in my head. I don't know what it is. The doctors think it is epilepsy. And I have tablets against epilepsy. But I am not cured.

G.v.W.: How did you know (Croiset's) name?

Fosbakk: Up there was an officer in NATO from Holland. He knew about Croiset and gave it to my brother who had the same (trouble) in his head. My brother, a businessman, went to Croiset a year ago and my brother is fine.

G.v.W.:   The treatment was successful ?

Fosbakk: Yes.

G.v.W.:   (to the camera) When this gentleman entered Mr Croiset's room, Mr Croiset said immediately, (*translating*) 'I see something wrong in your head . . . that causes pressure . . . heavy . . . that he can collapse . . . I never tell a patient You are an epileptic because I never know whether he knows . . . I treat this man and he flies back tonight to Norway . . . And from now on my treatment will be long distance treatment for three months. Then I ask whether it has been successful. If it's successful, then I continue. If not, I stop.'

The older of the two Norwegians then produced an envelope containing a photograph of a young girl :

G.v.W.:   The older gentleman has a letter with him. I see a portrait. (*Croiset looks at the photograph*)

Croiset: (*G.v.W. translating*) This young girl has a disease in her brain which causes pressure on her balance organ. According to my opinion, it's not epilepsy but a pressure on her organ of balance . . . She doesn't lose consciousness . . . I try to help her, but it will be difficult.

I have given a sample of the many patients who attended Croiset's clinic during our filming sessions. Now I want to deal with a patient whose illness and death were described to us by a Doctor Veldman, a general practitioner who practises in Enschede and who knew Gerard Croiset when the clairvoyant lived there. When interviewed by Doctor Pickard, Doctor

Veldman declared that he had experience of Croiset's successful *diagnoses* by clairvoyance but was at pains to point out that
the *healing* was quite a different matter. Dr Veldman gave an
example of Croiset's clairvoyant diagnosis from a number of
blood smears. Veldman said, 'He (Croiset) took the blood
smears in his hand, and he said "This is of a man, (this is) of a
woman who has (such and such) a diease." And besides that, he
told many things about the life of the patient, but only by
induction of the blood smear.'

Dr Pickard:	He had actually to touch it ? Did he use the microscope ?
Dr Veldman:	No. Only to touch.
G.v.W.:	Did *you* know what the patient had ?
Dr Veldman:	No, I didn't know. A colleague gave me the smears. The colleague himself didn't know ... only his assistant knew. He had the list numbered.
Dr Pickard:	In a code form ?
Dr Veldman:	In a code form – and the assistant of the doctor only knew what it was.
G.v.W.:	So telepathy is almost excluded ... He couldn't be reading your mind ?
Dr Veldman:	It is a double blind.
Dr Pickard:	And how often is he right with his diagnoses?
Dr Veldman:	Very often. He is very good.
G.v.W.:	Could you make an estimate ?
Dr Veldman:	80 per cent ; many times, 90 per cent.
G.v.W.:	Isn't that astonishing, Dr Pickard ?
Dr Pickard:	It is. It's more than many doctors. (*Laughter*) How detailed is Mr Croiset in his diagnoses ? Does he for example say 'Oh! There's something wrong with this man's leg or this man's knee', or does he actually describe the disease – like 'poliomyelitis' – and say which muscles are actually involved ?

Dr Veldman:	He was many times very detailed. He mentioned quite just the disease.
G.v.W.:	And what are his descriptions like ? Does he use medical terms, or have you got to interpret his description into medical terms in order to understand them ?
Dr Veldman:	Yes, medical terms ... weren't always right ... many times half and half.
Dr Pickard:	Yes, I found that when talking to him too. But he says enough to make it obvious what he is trying to get at.
Dr Veldman:	Oh yes.
Dr Pickard:	But can you tell us of an actual case when he used his clairvoyant powers to make a surprising diagnosis that perhaps you wouldn't have known on your own ?
Dr Veldman:	Yes. It was the case of a painter staying in his house, and one night Mr Croiset phoned me and said, 'Will you come immediately to me ? This man is awfully tight on his chest and he's spitting blood and you must come! You should come at once!' And when I was in the car I thought that it's medical nonsense what he tells me – he had said the heart valves of the patient were away – *he had no heart valves.*
Dr Pickard:	Do you mean .. ?
Dr Veldman:	They'd disappeared.
Dr Pickard:	Not all of them, surely ?
Dr Veldman:	His lungs were filling with blood and in the car I thought 'That is a medical nonsense'. But when I came there was a man with an awfully tight chest and spitting blood and I have immediately sent him to hospital ... It was very difficult to get him out of the attack. After six weeks suddenly the man died. We never made a right diagnosis.

Dr Pickard: You just didn't know what was the matter ?

Dr Veldman: No, we didn't know what it was. I was in hospital with cardiologists and treated him for cardiac asthma ... but we didn't really know what had gone wrong. The heart was enlarged, was to left and to right enlarged. Otherwise, no abnormal heart murmurs ... We asked to make a post-mortem. By the opening of the heart we found that the mitral valves were completely eaten away by an endocarditis, by an inflammation of the valves.

Dr Pickard: There was no sign of mitral valve left at all ?

Dr Veldman: No. Completely eaten away.

Dr Pickard: So that's why you heard no murmur, because it didn't stop the blood flowing out ?

G.v.W.: So Croiset had been right completely ?

Dr Veldman: Completely right from the beginning.

When asked to comment on Croiset's powers of healing as opposed to diagnosis, Dr Veldman said :

Dr Veldman: I think the healing powers of Mr Croiset are a psychological influence and ... art of suggestion.

Dr Pickard: But are you quite sure that he does have some healing powers ?

Dr Veldman: Sure ... many. But the explanation of that healing is psychological.

Dr Pickard: What sort of cases have you seen him help to cure ?

Dr Veldman: Neurological cases, poliomyelitis, psychosomatic diseases, asthma, blood pressure and stomach diseases.

Dr Pickard: But ... they're not just psychosomatic conditions. I mean poliomyelitis isn't a psychosomatic condition ?

G*

Dr Veldman: No, no, no. I think neurological and psycho-somatic diseases.

Dr Pickard: You said *suggestion*, Dr. Veldman ; but what about animals ? He is healing paralysed dogs, for instance, and horses.

Dr Veldman: I believe so. When he treats a dog, the people in the surroundings of the dog believe them-selves otherwise and that has an influence on the dog.

In trying to sum up her own impressions of Croiset as a healer, Dr Christine Pickard said :

Like Dr Veldman, I can't begin to understand how Mr Croiset manages his extraordinary feats of healing. But I saw enough to be convinced that he does manage it. If someone had asked me to believe in X-rays before they were dis-covered I would have said they were nonsense. But they exist, and I'm prepared to acknowledge that there is some-thing more in this than we understand at the moment. I saw many cases and I was convinced that (Croiset) had really a tremendous power to improve the health of these people. Take the case of the thatcher, the man who fell off roof tops because he kept getting unbalancing attacks. He was found to have a tumour on the brain. The doctors who saw it there thought they could do nothing when he fell over. Mr Croiset managed to treat him and the fits have completely stopped now. This is something that can't be explained by ordinary means. Croiset does a lot to improve the quality of people's lives rather than the quantity. That is, he doesn't just set out to prolong life. He makes sure, or tries to, that the individual patient has as good a time of it as possible on this earth. His headaches are made less, his aches and pains are reduced. He can walk. He can eat normally. These are all important things and we ought to try and do this more rather than give (the patient) an extra two years at the end of his life . . . But as a final plea I would like to ask you and especially doctors, who need to do research into this field, to have an open mind and to look at this phenomenon before they condemn it.

Before I describe the final clairvoyant test to which we subjected Gerard Croiset, and which was to have been the climax of our film, I ought to try and summarise my own conclusions arising from Croiset's healing.

The cases I saw for myself or heard described with unimpeachable evidence included examples of diagnosis by clairvoyance, by psychometry and possibly by mind-reading. Of the three kinds of extra-sensory perception, mind-reading is perhaps the most difficult to test and yet the one which appears to have won general acceptance – we are all prepared to believe in, even to quote personal experience of, telepathy. Yet I do not see how the evidence of Dr Veldman for clairvoyance in the cases of the blood samples and the man 'with no heart valves' can be reasonably refuted. In these examples, Croiset was demonstrating a power to perceive by 'extra-sensory perception' a state of affairs persisting at the time – he was not 'seeing into the future'. This is extraordinary enough and in our present state of knowledge, we are not able to say how it is done. When we are confronted with clairvoyance which involves pre-cognition of future events, the difficulties of acceptance let alone explanation are even greater: for who wants to believe these days in predestination ?

Nevertheless, one should follow wherever the evidence leads no matter how absurd the conclusion may at present appear to be. What reasonable theory can be put forward to explain clairvoyance as demonstrated by Croiset in the 'blood samples' and 'no heart valves' cases ?

Normal human perception requires an organ of perception such as an eye, ear, tongue or nose. The reliability and keenness of these organs varies from person to person and even in one and the same person at different times. The older we get, the more restricted becomes our perception of hearing and vision (to take two of the most obvious failings). For instance, the high pitched radar squeak of a bat heard in youth fails to register by the time most people are over twenty-five. Still, the stimulus is there ; the bat has not stopped squeaking. When the stimulus *is* capable of activating the organ of perception, the perceptions are then translated into recognisable form by various areas of the brain. It would therefore seem logical to conclude that what we call extra-sensory perception is in reality a sensory perception via an organ at present not recognised and the sensations are translated by an area of the brain at present not localised. We are all aware of the remains in our bodies of atrophied organs which once performed a useful function, for example, the coccyx (or human remains of a tail) and the appendix. When I was a young man at university, I was friendly for three years with another young fellow who went into hospital for the removal of an egg! This egg, I believe, is still kept in pickle in the university medical school. The Rev. A—— (he was later ordained into the Church of England) had as part of his anatomy the atrophied remnants of a bird's egg-producing apparatus. Why then should Croiset and similar clairvoyants not be endowed with an organ which allows them to perceive through space – and even time ?

It should not be beyond human ingenuity to devise experiments to detect whether this theory of an organ of clairvoyance and a localised brain area for the translating of the perceptions is true or false. Could the presumed organ be that mysterious gland, the pineal, whose function is at present unknown ?

Such a suggestion may not be as fantastic as at first it might seem. In New Zealand there still exists a 'living fossil', a lizard which ought to have become extinct 140,000,000 years ago, along with the other members of his order, the Rhynocephalia. As it is, the olive green tuatura, a lizard reaching a length of over two feet, retains an astonishing anatomical feature: on the top of its skull is the vestiges of *a third eye.* This is called the pineal gland and is found in the higher vertebrates, in man for instance, situated deep in the brain. The all-seeing eye ?

As to Croiset's ability or otherwise to cure diseases, reliable conclusions are just as difficult to arrive at. Animal ailments appear to a layman to be broadly classifiable into two categories: first, those caused by interference from outside the body by other living organisms or by accident, second those ailments brought upon the body by the mind – the so-called psychosomatic ailments. Croiset does not claim to cure every disease. He will not touch cancer. When he diagnosed the case of 'no heart valves' he realised his limitations and urgently summoned a doctor – Dr Veldman. Veldman thought Croiset's diagnosis was fantastic in its error ; when the patient died after conventional medical treatment, an autopsy proved Croiset to have been correct.

The daily workings of the animal body from blood circulation to digestion, from regeneration of the tissues to excretion of waste are a function of the subconscious part of the mind: 'who, by taking thought can add one cubit to his stature?' So, ultimately is the 'curing' of ailments: without being conscious of it, we cure ourselves.

Nevertheless, all men die. It is obvious that the subconscious physician in all of us is not infallible or indeed consistent, for it works better in some people than in others. Doctors who have studied Croiset, and who are prepared to accept that he is not a charlatan, appear to believe that he works by what they call 'suggestion' – presumably by influencing and stimulating a person's 'subconscious physician'. This may indeed be a large part of the explanation, but it does not fully explain his 'cures' of subjects not susceptible to suggestion – animals or children, or adults whose atrophied muscles he appears to make move by an unseen power – the same power perhaps as moved the T-shaped rods in the war-time film.

People who take the study of parapsychology seriously believe that Gerard Croiset's major contribution to that kind of research is his celebrated 'chair test'. This is because the 'chair test' as an experiment has the one quality that scientists insist on before they will accept results – it can be repeated.

Of course, human beings are illogical, and scientists are human beings – need one complete the syllogism ? At any rate, not many scientists appear to be convinced by Croiset's chair test since it demonstrates that rum manifestation *clairvoyance*, and not only that, clairvoyance which foretells the future – precognition. If you accept precognition then all its other disreputable cronies want to elbow their way into the laboratory too, such as Fate, Kismet, Predestination, Divine

Providence, even ; in the end Man has to surrender his Free Will. I don't know any scientist who is ready to accept that.

The test was devised by Professor Tenhaeff more than 20 years ago, and up to date has been repeated hundreds of times in different countries: in fact, so many times that we felt Croiset was getting bored with it. Basically the set-up is simple. Croiset makes a series of predictions about a person, at the time unknown, who will sit in a designated chair at a meeting to be called in the future any time from an hour to six weeks after the predictions. I say 'six weeks' because that was the length of time which elapsed in our own experiment for the Croiset film: for anything I know to the contrary, he may be able to foretell indefinitely into the future. What would really be interesting would be to ask Gerard Croiset to make a chair test prediction say thirty or forty years into the future (when he and the rest of us would have died) for the edification of those who come after us. The mechanics of the experiment are straight-forward: Croiset's prognostications must be recorded and kept secret and the choosing of the person who is to sit in the 'chair' must be in the hands of an independent agency which will preclude any collusion. At the given time, that is when the subject is safely in the chair, the forecasts are made public and checked to see whether they do in fact relate to the subject.

A description of our chair test will make the procedure plain. We enlisted the help of the Dutch Society for Psychical Research. On 14 April 1967, at Hilversum, Bob Saunders filmed two predictions by Croiset in the presence of two reput-able witnesses, Mr W. C. A. Francissen, a Hague lawyer, Vice-President of the Dutch Society for Psychical Research, and a Catholic priest. Croiset began his predictions know-ing that a meeting would be called six weeks later, on 26 May, at the small Pulchri Studio in the Hague, organised by the Dutch Society for Psychical Research on behalf of the BBC ; he also knew that some people sitting in the first two rows of chairs in the Pulchri Studio would hold a number from 1 to 24. Croiset was to make a prediction about a person whose number would not be chosen until the audience was already seated six weeks later on 26 May. Several stages would be gone through before the final number was arrived at ; the last stage in choosing the number was to be left to the BBC. No matter what happened before, we believed we had devised a way which would rule out any chance of collusion.

On the occasion of the filming of his prediction in Hilversum on 14 April, somewhat to Saunders' dismay, Croiset made two predictions – one concerning a man, the other a woman. For a number of reasons Saunders decided not to use the predictions about the man for the purpose of our film. Croiset himself felt uncertain about the predictions he had made concerning the man. Then we only had the footage and time for one subject and the predictions about the woman seemed more interesting.

When the camera started rolling on the occasion of the predictions in Hilversum, Mr Francissen began by saying, 'Now in a few moments the experiment will start, and remember this is April the 14th, Friday, and the exact time is 8 minutes past 5.'

Croiset : I am now going to give you a picture of what I am seeing concerning a person who will be present in Pulchri Studio in the Hague on the 26 May. I hope that the chair number will be selected by means of the cards.

I see at the moment a person who is very fit and well and jovial. She walks so quickly that when she came into a hall (it could be a theatre) she went along a row in order to sit down and tripped over the legs of the people already there.

The impression I get is that she has lived for a short time near a park in which there is a little house with cracks in its outside walls. I will draw the house. See, here's the wall and in this wall there is a large crack. It seems to me that it is situated in a green or park.

I often have to be on the third floor and I am generally there with 4 and often 5 people at home. Among them is a young boy, a nice little chap about three years old with dark hair cut short. This little boy has just managed in some way to make a hole in the material covering his right leg.

When I leave the house and go to the right there is a park.

If I go to the left there is a very high building on top of which are some large letters. It seems to me – well, I won't go into much detail – They're letters about 1 metre high and 30 centimetres broad. When I stand there, then to the right I look at a building which has a small annexe with a yellow covered roof.

This person has visited a large department store where there were piles of cloth from which she had selected a bluish coloured cloth with white polka dots, and when she came home she realised she didn't like it.

They have visited a diamond merchant, possibly a jeweller's. They tried to buy a ring, but the ring they wanted wouldn't fit over the finger joint.

They've recently talked about fitting wainscoting into the home. What has this discussion been about wainscoting ?

I see at the moment a farm in Israel. It has got in some way to be defended. Has there been an attack on a Kibbutz? That's what they're called, aren't they ? Well, an Israel type farm. I got a very strong feeling about that.

I've just recently been in a block of flats. This block of flats has a staircase of reinforced concrete, but there's also a balustrade. One of the spokes is broken through. I get a powerful feeling that a child is trying to squeeze through the gap.

I see at the moment a party cake with very thin candles. One of them is yellow. What kind of feelings have there been with that thin yellow candle ?

Thank you very much for your attention and I hope very much that the experiment will succeed.

As the audience filed in through the doors of the Puchri Studio in the Hague on 26 May 1967, twenty-four of them, at random, were handed a printed ticket from an adding machine worked at the time by Mr Francissen the lawyer. A Dutch clergyman standing by Francissen indicated by chance, as the spirit moved him, which of the public was to be handed a numbered ticket. People who received tickets were asked to sit anywhere in the first two rows.

Further to rule out collusion I had myself proposed a method of choosing the number which would be the final stage in the choice. Croiset wanted the number to be chosen by means of twenty-four cards which would be shuffled by a volunteer from the audience. I agreed to this but said the ultimate choice of the card must be left to the BBC team. What I had arranged was that one of our colleagues in London, Ivan Lockett, would put a phone call through to the Hague at 8.30 pm on 26 May, when we expected (i) our audience would be seated, 24 of them with numbered tickets ; (ii) we should have shown on a large screen the sound-film of Croiset's predictions six weeks before. Then Lockett would phone us a number. That number would be the difference in millibars between the maximum and the minimum barometric pressure recorded that day in London.

At about 8 pm the proceedings in the Pulchri Studio were opened by our presenter Gerton van Wageningen and the Dutch camera crews filmed what went on. First the film of Croiset's two predictions was shown.

Our audience waited expectantly. Either Croiset's predictions had been successful and two people sitting in the first two rows were experiencing some very mixed feelings – or perhaps he had been successful with one and not the other – or maybe the whole thing was a flop.

At 8.30 pm the telephone on Gerton van Wageningen's table on the dais in front of the projection screen rang and the following conversation took place :

G.v.Wageningen: Hello, good evening, who are you ?
Voice: BBC London.
G.v.W.: Thank you and what are you going to tell me ?
Voice: Oh just a moment. Mr Lockett is coming on the line.
G.v.W.: Thank you. Hello, good evening, this is Pulchri.
Lockett: Here in London it's just after 8.30 pm.
G.v.W.: Just after 8.30 pm. That's correct. Correct.
Lockett: On 26 May.

185

G.v.W.: 26 May.

Lockett: And the maximum barometric difference in London so far today is 8 millibars.

G.v.W.: 8 millibars. May I repeat? The maximum barometric difference in London today is 8 millibars. Is that correct?

Lockett: That is correct.

Having elicited the random number 8, Gerton van Wageningen turned back to the audience and said, 'Ladies and gentlemen, I would like to ask now the co-operation of one volunteer from the audience but not anyone from the first two rows. What I would like the Volunteer to do is to come here, shuffle a number of cards, twenty-four cards which are here, and then take the eight first cards away and show to the camera the number which is on the ninth card.'

Eventually a young lady stepped up on to the dais, shuffled the cards and showed the next following card. It was number fifteen. 'May I ask him or her to make him or herself known please?'

A man stood up. Van Wageningen then said, 'We heard that Mr Croiset was not too confident in his first experiment concerning the man. Now, since you are Mr 15 would you please tell me how many per cent according to your estimation of Mr Croiset's prediction is correct?' The man with number 15 replied in Dutch and van Wageningen said, 'Some 30 per cent. But was there one detail that struck you particularly in his prediction?' Again the man replied in Dutch and van Wageningen translated into English; 'Yes, the detail that struck me particularly was about the house and the garden and the hedge and the border with earth . . . I wore a blue shirt that day. We went from the Hague to Wassenaar in order to look for a new house. The new house was under construction and I had to creep through a gate and then I fell. I saw a door with a window broken and I tried to come through but didn't succeed and my wife and everybody laughed about me behaving like an acrobat. That's quite correct.'

Besides conducting a chair test, we were of course making a film, and for a film in English, a subject who only spoke Dutch was something of an obstacle. We asked Gerton to pass on to choosing a second number. He addressed the audience and said, 'As you have heard, Mr Croiset did actually make two predictions on 14 April: one involving a man and one involving a woman. Now may I ask you Madam (addressing the volunteer from the audience) to draw a second card ?' The volunteer did as she was asked and the number eighteen turned up. Gerton van Wageningen then asked 'Who has number eighteen ?' A lady sitting on the right of the hall indicated that she had the number. Her name was Mrs Scholten, and van Wageningen began to question her.

He asked first if Croiset's predictions were correct and Mrs Scholten said that apart from some details, the majority were. Van Wageningen then asked if she had tripped over the legs of people when coming into the Pulchri Studios. At this, Croiset interrupted and instructed van Wageningen to confine himself to asking whether the predictions were correct or not. This seemed to be a justifiable request, for the interrogator was clearly jumping to conclusions and Mrs Scholten may well have tripped up in some other place – as indeed she had. She said that visiting what she called by its Dutch name, a *bioskop,* a cinema some three weeks before, she had tripped over the legs of people already sitting there.

Van Wageningen then asked Mrs Scholten some general questions and the description of events leading to her coming to our meeting shook me when I first heard them. Mrs Scholten was diffident about speaking English and her sister, a Mrs Kersbergen who had come with her, told the story. Mrs Kersbergen said,

> Well, my sister told me that her sister-in-law, *who is a patient of Mr Croiset,*[1] came here (to Mrs Scholten's home at Zuitmeer near the Hague) and asked, 'Can you drive me to the Hague, to Pulchri Studio ?' My sister said, 'I'm very

[1] My italics

busy, the children are not yet in bed . . .' and so on. Then she asked her husband several times, and he said, 'I'm busy too.' So she said 'O.K. . . ' (7 o'clock I believe it was), 'All right. I go with you.'

When I heard this, it seemed to me damaging that our subject appeared to have this link with Croiset, no matter how fortuitous and tenuous it might be. She *had* been brought to the meeting (much against her inclination, as I believe implicitly) by a sister-in-law who was linked to Croiset in that she was his patient. Yet at the same time, if there had been any collusion, it had been done in a very cliff-hanging way, leaving the bringing of the subject to the hall right up to the eleventh hour. Then again, I could not see how the subject could have been successfully engineered by an outsider over all the other obstacles of numbers from adding machines, the chance of handing out of numbers at the door of the hall, the shuffling of the cards and the choice of a number from London which would be necessary before she could obtain the right number to choose her as the one person fitting Croiset's prophecies. For she *did* fit them – *almost without exception.*

We checked Croiset's prophecies about 'Madam 18' in two ways: first, van Wageningen went over them at the time in the Pulchri Studio, then some days later on 1 June, a camera crew filmed sequences at Mrs Scholten's home in Zuitemeer. Croiset's clairvoyant perceptions in this experiment fall into three categories:

    (i) perception of states of affairs already existing or events which had already happened when the prophecies were made.

    (ii) perception of events which had not taken place when Croiset made his prophecies.

    (iii) perception of a state of mind known only to Mrs Scholten.

From the point of view of a convincing scientific experiment, the second and third categories are obviously the more valuable as ruling out any collusion. Out of at least nineteen correct prophecies about Mrs Scholten, four prophecies fall into these categories. Before I discuss them I will set out Croiset's statements about the person having number eighteen.

Prophecy	Comment
1. A woman	correct
2. Very fit, well and jovial	correct
3. *She tripped over the legs of people in a hall or theatre	correct – but happened 3 weeks after the prophecy
4. She lives near a park	correct
5. In the park is a small house with cracks in the outside wall	correct
6. The dwelling is on the 3rd floor	correct
7. She has 4 or 5 people in her home	correct. Mrs Scholten had 4 people and was expecting a baby in 3 months
8. One of the household is a boy of three with dark cropped hair	correct. Mrs Scholten's son, Lucas
9. The little boy has torn the right leg of his trousers	correct
10. When one leaves the house there is a park to the right	correct
11. To the left of the house stands a very high building with large letters	correct
12. Looking to the right one sees an annexe with a yellow roof	correct

189

13. Subject visited department store, bought bluish material with white polka dots — Mrs Scholten said the material was green – otherwise correct

14. The material bought at the shop was disliked after being taken home — correct

15. Subject visited jewellers and tried to buy a ring which didn't fit — Mrs Scholten's sister-in-law bought toy rings for little girls and Mrs Scholten tried one which didn't fit

16. *Talk about fitting wainscoting in the home — Mrs Scholten saw an advertisement for wainscoting in a magazine and intended talking to her husband about it but never got around to it. She merely thought about it

17. *A farm in Israel ... has there been an attack on a Kibbutz ? — Mrs Scholten denied any connection with Israel. Four days after the Pulchri Studio chair test the headline in one of the Dutch papers read: ATTACK ON KIBBUTZ. A copy of this paper appeared on a table in Mrs Scholten's home on the morning of the BBC filming

18. *Block of flats with staircase of reinforced concrete ... a balustrade. One of the spokes broken ... a child is trying to squeeze through the gap — Mrs Scholten agreed there was a block of flats opposite her home with a balustrade but no broken spokes. She could see this from her room including a door with a pane missing. She wondered often whether a tiny child could climb through the space in the door and thrust itself through the balustrade spokes

190

19. A party cake with very thin candles. One of them is yellow	Mrs Scholten's nephew had a birthday party in the beginning of April. There were three candles one of which was yellow. The yellow candle stood out from the others because it would not fit into the holder. A lighted match was used to heat the holder in an attempt to make the candle fit

Does Gerard possess the astonishing clairvoyant powers which this chair test would indicate that he does ? Because I believe a transparently honest answer to this question is of the utmost importance I shall first take up the position of the Devil's Advocate and point out possible flaws in the case for clairvoyancy.

In the first place, we discovered by chance at the last moment that the lady with number eighteen, Mrs Scholten, had been brought to the Pulchri Studio by her sister-in-law, a patient of Mr Croiset's. It is possible that collusion between the sister-in-law and Croiset (without Mrs Scholten's knowledge) could have taken place. *If* the sister-in-law had known of all the incidents which follow, she could have retailed them to Croiset: they are numbers 1, 2, 4, 5, 6, 7, 8, 9, 10, 11, 12, 13, 14, and 19. *If* Mrs Scholten also had been a party to the collusion then Croiset could have known about numbers 16 and 18, because although these only took place in Mrs Scholten's *thoughts,* she could have described her thoughts to her sister-in-law and so to Croiset.

We are then left with items number 3 and 17. Number 3 concerned Mrs Scholten's tripping over people's feet as she went into a cinema which took place three weeks after Croiset's prophecy had already been recorded on film. Of course, we could argue that Mrs Scholten was fully a party to a conspiracy and was lying about the incident to make it fit in with the prophecy. Item number 17 concerned the attack on a Kibbutz (an actual newspaper headline) an incident in the notorious Six Days War when Egypt, without warning, made war on Israel fully six weeks after Croiset had made his chair test prophecies.

I now drop the cloak of Devil's Advocate and set out my own convictions. Having tested Croiset myself with the Sir John Franklin letter, and having received unimpeachable testimony in the case of the blood samples and the man with 'no heart valves', I believe there was no collusion whatsoever in our own chair test and that the fact that Mrs Scholten was brought to the Pulchri Studio by a Croiset patient was fortuitous. I think that the 'attack on Kibbutz' is an absolutely water-tight piece of evidence as are other numbers which I have starred, namely 3 (which demonstrates precognition on the part of Croiset) and numbers 16 and 18 (which show a perception by Croiset of Mrs Scholten's thoughts – telepathy). On this showing, I have no hesitation in accepting the remainder of the 19 items, and declare my belief that Croiset's was an astonishing feat, for everything he said was virtually correct – a hundred percent performance.

Of course, there is a much more startling conclusion to which one might come and that is that some power wielded by Gerard Croiset, possibly unconsciously, led to Mrs Scholten's sister-in-law (again unknowingly) being moved to take Mrs Scholten to the Pulchri Studio in order that she could fulfil the role of the lady in the prophecy!

7
What Does
It Mean?

For the last quarter of a century I have been tantalised by my contacts with so-called psi-phenomena. I began my story in chapter 1 by rattling off a list of these phenomena – 'apparitions, poltergeists, possession, clairvoyance, mind-reading, pre-cognition, stigmata, spirit-photographs and such-like oddities.' The reader who has patiently followed me this far is probably just as curious as I am to know what it all means.

Let me start by trying to lay a simple but firm foundation on which to build up an argument. I believe most people in their lifetime have come into contact with one or more of the oddities mentioned above. Nearly always they dismiss the experiences or happenings as being *subjective* – they have imagined them. So the foundation stone of the argument must depend on the answer 'yes' being given to the question – are any or all of such phenomena *objective* ?

There are so many reputable witnesses down the years to poltergeist phenomena that we should be unscientific if we did not accept that noises and movements of objects have been produced objectively in ways which physics is unable to explain at present. Again, so many reputable witnesses have seen with their own eyes and photographed and filmed bodily stigmata – whether those of Padre Pio with his five bleeding wounds of Christ, a 'George' with his barbed-wire scratches, neck rope-mark and so on – that such stigmata have to be accepted as objective. It is no use doctors and psychiatrists explaining away stigmata as the result of 'hysterical' states in the victim. That explanation explains nothing. The blunt fact is that nobody knows just how stigmata are produced and (in my opinion) they must therefore be put in the same category as the unexplained noises and movements associated with poltergeist victims. Next, take clairvoyance: the experiments of scientists like Professor Tenhaeff over many years with men and women like Gerard Croiset have proved beyond reasonable doubt that certain gifted people are able to 'see' across space and time without benefit of eyes. Once again, we don't know how it is done, and being denied such knowledge our first reaction as reasonable human beings is to explain away this 'miracle' as faking.

Our adult human predicament is this: such phenomena as I have so far mentioned have the appearance of miracles, but we cannot accept miracles; children (and poets) of course, can. And yet for hundreds of thousands of years Man had to accept the sun, moon and stars, the earth, the sea and tides without having the remotest idea of how they 'worked' even. They are indeed wonderful, more wonderful perhaps than psi-phenomena, but nonetheless accepted as objective by all human beings. Now, we in our turn are forced to accept poltergeist phenomena, clairvoyance and many other unexplained psi-phenomena because they, like Everest, like the sun, moon and stars, are *there*.

For myself, I believe such phenomena do exist objectively; as to whether there is an after-life or not my position is one of agnosticism. At this stage, I believe it is inadmissible to offer psi-phenomena as an argument for life after death because, simply, we have not yet exhausted explanations of these phenomena which present-day physics will accommodate.

In previous chapters I have occasionally indicated my own tentative opinions as to what might be profitable directions into which to research for explanations. What I shall now attempt is the pursuit of such explanations with the endeavour to formulate if possible a unified theory into which they might all fit.

The first thing to notice is that all the phenomena are connected in some way with man's brain: when a poltergeist focus is asleep, silence reigns, objects stop flying about, the phenomena cease; when a person sees an apparition it is not the eye which apprehends it, but the brain; when the five bleeding wounds of Christ appear on the body of a holy nun or priest it is not the hands and feet and side which cause the stigmata, but the brain; when a clairvoyant has visions through time and space his eyes are not the seer, his brain is. The brain has a powerful function in the production of psi-phenomena.

But is the brain the prime mover in the production of such phenomena? If the brain is drained of blood for two minutes or more, it dies or is irreparably injured, so it is not an entirely independent organ. Again, if the brain is denied certain chemicals normally carried to it in the blood from the mysterious ductless glands, thyroid secretion for instance from the thyroid gland, the brain malfunctions and its possessor becomes a cretin.

The brain, like any other physical component of the human body, continually changes its substance. Sir Charles Dodds, writing in the *British Medical Journal* (2 December 1950) reported:

> In the case of man the total turnover of protein occurred in about 80 days, while the liver and serum proteins were turned over in 10 days and the lung, brain, bone, skin and principal muscle in 158 days ... It is a rather terrifying thought that the whole of the protein in the human body is replaced in roughly 160 days, and at the present time we can only speculate on the mechanism controlling this elaborate re-synthesis.

Sir Charles Sherrington, distinguished physiologist and author of *Man On His Nature* wrote:

> The circulation of the blood (is) always going forward. Where each artery plunges into the brain, a little whirlpool of blood is visible. This brings home to us how very eagerly the brain breathes. The brain is, of course, a corporeal thing and composed like other body organs of just physico-

chemical stuff, which breaks down finally into waste products.[1]

The brain is . . . a corporeal thing and composed like other body organs of just physico-chemical stuff, which breaks down finally into waste products. The brain, then, 'dies' every day, but the 'me' who employs the brain does not: 'I' only die once. I cannot escape the conclusion, therefore, that brain and I are two separate entities. What no one knows for certain at present is whether the total extinction of the brain brings with it the total extinction of 'me'; because while in my earthly lifetime I am using my brain to express myself, neither I nor anyone else can yet *prove* that the 'I' can continue to express itself through some other mode and can therefore exist independently. Or, for that matter, disprove it.

Possession is a very interesting phenomenon in this respect, for if we could prove its objective existence it would mean that the 'I' of one person can briefly take over the brain of another. This would not necessarily prove life after death, for we should first of all have to dismiss another psi-phenomenon, telepathy. In the cases from my own experience which I have cited in this book I believe there is one genuine example of telepathy, when Mrs Hockley said the word *batayiē* immediately before I did: her 'me' got the information from my 'me' in a manner unknown to physics, and at the time, the two 'me's' were alive in the sense that the brains through which they were expressing themselves were alive. When Mrs Hockley appeared to submit her brain as a vehicle for Jan Masaryk or Gandhi, the brains of both men (as Sherrington put it) had 'finally broken down into waste products.' Whether their 'me's' had a continuing independent existence is unproven by Mrs Hockley's behaviour. The most economical explanation of her performances is that the knowledge she showed of Masaryk's fall from the balcony or of Gandhi's being shot and cremated had been acquired by normal means, retained in her memory and resuscitated in trance under the guise of a secondary personality. I am not

[1]New York Times Magazine 4 December 1949.

saying that this *is* the explanation, only that without further evidence it is the only one we can accept.

In the same way 'George's' trance-possession by 'Biggs', by other characters in the airforce episodes and by 'Alfreda', where they *can* be explained appear to be most economically explained by assuming that his 'me' was making use of information acquired over the years by normal means and dredged up from his subconscious to be expressed in a series of secondary personalities. Again, I am not saying this *is* the explanation, for without arduous research and experimentation we are merely speculating, merely groping in the dark. I have said I do not believe that 'George' or anyone else faked the spirit-photographs. Research showed that the particular film we used, Kodak Plus-X, could have registered an ultra-violet image not visible to the human eye. But there is in fact another possible explanation, and that is that George's 'me' could have directly imposed an image on the film. There appears to be a case for such a phenomenon. In 1910 Professor T. Fukurai of Kohyassan University first claimed that pictures could be transferred by certain people to sealed photographic plates without the use of light or a lens.[1] An American, Dr Jule Eisenbud MD, recently published his account of Ted Serios, a man who could apparently transfer mental pictures to film.[2] If the 'me' controlling the brain of Gerard Croiset could make steel divining rods turn at a distance, or cause atrophied muscles to agitate without physical contact, I see nothing inherently impossible about a photographic emulsion being affected by the same or similar powers. But once again, we do not have to call up spirits from the vasty deep to furnish ourselves with an explanation: physics must surely one day explain the phenomenon.

If we are ever to prove the existence of life after death, I believe that apparitions of the dead are the one phenomenon likely to offer proof. The first requisite, the *sine qua non*, is to catch your ghost. My own contacts with apparitions are Mrs

[1]Clairvoyance and Thoughtography – T. Fukurai, Rider & Co. London 1931.
[2]*The World of Ted Serios* – Jule Eisenbud, William Morrow and Co., New York. 1967.

Hockley's Ralph Bathurst; the Ardara Avenue spook; the 'him' seen by George in what to the rest of those present and to the film camera was an empty chair; and the two apparitions at Northfleet seen by Mrs Maxted and Mr Essex. In every case, only one person at any one time saw the ghost. There is no witness to corroborate that the ghost was objectively there and in the instance where more than one person was present (or awake) only one 'saw' the ghost. This might be taken as proof that the apparitions were subjective illusions, but such cannot be an inexorable conclusion, for the Ardara Avenue spook was seen by three different people at different times just as the Northfleet ghost was seen by two separate persons. If we accept my theory of a receptor in the brain, such as the pineal gland, able to apprehend super-sensory phenomena, then while this allows ghosts an objective existence and a manner of being seen according to a law of physics not yet understood, it still does not prove that ghosts are spirits of the dead: they may well be apparitions of the living.

The subject of the pineal gland is worth returning to. It is a ductless gland the size of a pea and shaped like a pine cone, hence its name. It is situated in the brain behind and above the pituitary gland which itself lies behind the root of the nose. The pineal gland is attached to the third ventricle of the brain; it contains pigment similar to that in the retina of the eye as well as tiny granules of what have been called 'brain sand.' What the gland secretes is unknown and the exact influence of the pineal secretion is still obscure though it is 'certainly not indispensible to life.'[1] There seems to be a case for suspecting that the pineal gland is most active in our childhood and atrophies as we become adult.

If I try to pull together the results of my twenty-five years experience of what is beyond belief, but perhaps not beyond trust, such results may appear meagre – but not as meagre as all that.

Have I seen apparitions? Yes. Have other people seen apparitions in my presence? Yes. Am I convinced of the truth

[1]F. Tilney MD. *The Pineal Gland.*

198

of witnesses who claim to have seen apparitions? The answer is yes – yes to all these questions, but that 'yes' does not prove the objective existence of spirits.

Have I experienced poltergeist phenomena? Again, the answer is yes: I have heard knockings, seen objects move without a physical explanation that I can adduce. Here I am on more certain ground for additional witnesses assure me that it was not my five wits playing me false. Manifestations of this type must surely be worthy of scientific investigation.

Have I experienced successful clairvoyance? Yes I have, with Croiset demonstrating to my satisfaction two varieties of clairvoyance, namely post-cognition with the Franklin letter and pre-cognition with the chair test.

Now, if I search for an explanation of these visitations and powers I don't get very far; but as I have said, our ancestors couldn't explain the sun, moon and stars, but they had to accept them because they were *there*. And so, although realising my own ignorance, I must acknowledge that I have experienced phenomena which cannot be dismissed simply because I am ignorant of their meaning or causation. I have to conclude that the human psyche has powers or can connect with and employ powers which are frightening in their intensity. Whether these powers are human, superhuman, good or evil or merely impersonal in human terms, I do not know. As human beings we are both curious about and fearful of the unknown. I believe that much of what goes under the blanket term of psi-phenomena must eventually be explained by natural laws. Everybody accepts gravity – what goes up must come down. But this law of gravity can easily be neutralised or at least modified: the Montgolfier brothers modified the power of gravity when they sent up their first hot-air balloon; birds flying modify gravity every day, so do air travellers; astronauts appear to achieve a state in which gravity is for all practical purposes neutralised. So why should I not accept that objects like George's floating oilcan do defy gravity and suspect that George and people like him are able to exert a neutralising influence on gravity with a form of energy that physics will one day explain ? I am certain that clairvoyance will be satisfactorily explained as perhaps a fairly rare but natural phenomenon. But on the other hand, who am I to deny the existence of a world beyond space and time which, after all are concepts created by man ? I am just as much in the dark as ever I was to know whether some of the powers I have sometimes been fearfully confronted with begin and end in finite Man. Experience says 'not proven' ; intuition says 'don't be too sure : there may well be that which is beyond belief.'